Skiing: CONDITIONING & TECHNIQUE

Gwen Rector Robinson

El Camino College
Torrance, California

NATIONAL PRESS BOOKS

Library of Congress Catalog Card Number: 73-91389
International Standard Book Numbers:
0-87484-278-6 (paper)
0-87484-279-4 (cloth)

Manufactured in the United States of America

National Press Books
850 Hansen Way, Palo Alto, California 94304

To
David,
Kim,
Stacey
and Mari

This book was set in Helvetica Light by Acme Type Company
and was printed by National Press. Sponsoring editor was
Richard W. Bare, and copy editor was Jeff Littleboy. Michelle
Hogan supervised production, and the book and cover were
designed by Nancy Sears.

Drawings on pages 38, 40, 44, 49, 51, 53, 59, 60, 62, and 66
are adapted from American Teaching Method by permission
of Dennis Sanford, Executive Director of the PSIA. © 1972 by
the Professional Ski Instructors of America.

Photographs on pages 33-58 are by Pete Wehrheim. Those
on pages 33, 34, 37, and 42 were taken at the Ski Racquet
Ski Shop in Torrance, California; the balance were taken in
Big Bear, California. Thanks to Randy Short, Director of the
Snow Summit Ski School, for demonstrating the techniques
illustrated in the Big Bear photographs.

CONTENTS

PREFACE

Purpose of this book is to compile basic knowledge and to describe skills necessary to the student of skiing for full enjoyment of the sport. Much of the information will be of value to even the most experienced skier. The author has attempted to include everything you've always wanted to know about skiing, but didn't know whom to ask.

Appreciation of skiing is enhanced by knowledge of the growth and development of the sport, as well as the roles and scope of organized skiing. Safety on the slopes, winter driving tips, and physical conditioning guidelines are included.

Skiing is one of the fastest growing recreational sports in America. It is particularly appealing to high school and college age students. Skiing differs in one aspect—it is not without danger. The hazards are quite real. Proper physical conditioning is highly important and, unfortunately, neglected by most skiers. Adequate instructions are essential before the novice can enjoy skiing without a high degree of hazard to his and others' safety.

The fundamentals of skiing cannot be learned properly without expert instruction. It is not a natural sport and cannot be learned by instinct. Studies have found that more than 74 percent of injured skiers have had no lessons. In this author's opinion, anyone of any age who has normal coordination, proper conditioning and continued instruction can safely enjoy skiing.

The popularity of skiing has developed to such a degree that the sport is being taught in many schools throughout the United States. For many years some of the larger universities have supported ski classes, clubs, and ski teams. Now, with the rapid growth of the sport, areas with snowmaking devices and artificial or simulated snow slopes are more available.

Television coverage of national and international skiing competitions is bringing ski racing to the public. Skiing has been named as one of the "lifetime sports" by the President's Council on Physical Fitness. The emphasis can be on family fun, or as an activity which allows anyone to engage in a thrilling competitive sport.

Chapter 1

A BRIEF HISTORY OF SKIING

Nobody knows how many times man slipped and slid on snow before he first got the idea of skiing. All we know is that the earliest ski was dug up in Sweden and is estimated to be 4,500 years old.

This one, called the Hoting Ski, is on display in the Swedish Ski Museum in Stockholm. There are a few other clues, such as stone carvings, which indicate that the first use of the ski was utilitarian—for hunting, migration and warfare.

At any rate, skiing as we know it was developed by the Scandinavians, and by 1795 all of Central Europe had been introduced to the technique. The sport didn't attract much attention in the United States until the Westward migration in 1849.

The word itself comes from the Norwegian *shee,* meaning "shoe." Clearly the ski afforded a quick, convenient utilitarian means of getting around on the snow. Three prehistoric types of skiing were known: the Arctic, Southern Arctic and Central Nordic.

The Arctic was like the Hoting ski, wide and short. It had four leather straps attached through holes to hold the foot securely, and the bottom was covered with animal hide. This type is still used in Siberia.

The Southern Arctic ski, developed after the Arctic,

was the forerunner of today's sports equipment. It looked like the ski of the 1930's—long, turned up at the tip, with raised footrests and wooden side-ridges. Southern Arctic skis were used in Scandinavia, Europe and west-central Russia.

Central Nordic skis were quite a bit different. The two skis were of unequal length. The left was about nine to 12 feet long, and was grooved for steering. The right was about seven or eight feet long and was covered with fur for traction. The grain of the fur was arranged for climbing traction on the hills—in other words, the same way the animal wore it, head to tail.

There were a couple of other primitive methods— one was the ancestor of today's oval webbed snowshoe; the other was just a pair of wooden slabs strapped to the feet.

The idea of skiing competition surfaced on both sides of the Atlantic in the middle years of the 19th century. In the U.S., mail carriers were the first to use skis, and men like the famous "Snowshoe" Thompson carried the mail on skis over the Sierra Nevada into California during the Gold Rush days. The miners, looking for any kind of action, decided to offer handsome prizes in gold for good performance, and so began the first American ski races in 1866.

In Norway about 1862, the first officially recorded ski competition was held. In 1877, the Christiana Ski Club was formed, from which the skiing maneuver "christy" gets its name.

During the 1880's ski jumping and cross-country competition became popular. The first U.S. ski club was organized at Ishpeming, Mich., in 1887. That town now is the home of the National Ski Hall of Fame and Ski Museum—worth a visit from any skier interested in mementoes from all over the world.

As you can imagine, literature on the art of skiing is considerable, but it is believed that the greatest influence came from a book written by Dr. Fridtjof Nansen, *The First Crossing of Greenland*. Nansen described how he adapted a rigid ski binding invented by the Norwegian Sondre Norheim and developed the turn known as the "telemark."

Two years after the toe iron was invented in 1894, Mathias Zdarsky devised the snowplow turn and produced the first analysis and descrip'ion of his Lillienfeld technque. Zdarsky's skis were too short, had no grooves and were unsteady for straight running. He also used a single pole with no "basket" or ring around the bottom for a brake. However, it was W. R. Rickmars, a Zdarsky fan, who wrote the first ski books in English.

In 1906, Zdarsky's Lillienfeld system became known as the Norwegian technique, utilizing stem and snowplow turns. Vivian Caulfield, an Englishman, in 1919, came up with an analysis of the sport which blasted Zdarsky's single-pole method. It is probable that Caulfield had a great deal to do with blending the Lillienfeld and pseudo-Norwegian techniques into the stickless stem turn and stem christy.

Austrian Hannes Schneider in 1925-26 wrote the first of a series of books describing what came to be known as the Arlberg technique. This was taught to the Austrian mountain troops in World War I and influenced the U.S.'s limited use of ski troops in World War II.

From mid-World War I to the mid-'20's, the open or scissors christy succeeded the telemark. It was in popular use in the U.S. until World War II.

Another Englishman, Sir Arnold Lunn, contributed his bit to the literature mainly in mountaineering techniques. During the early '30's, Sir Arnold was credited with the development of organized European skiing. At this time, turns were made by a stem and weight change; there was little body rotation and no sideslipping. But Sir Arnold's innovation, the slalom, was a hit and was adopted for Olympic competition.

The next big step forward came in 1928-30 when Austrian Rudolph Lettner invented and perfected the steel-edge ski. This enabled skiers to eliminate the deep-crouch position and revolutionized technique. This, coupled with Hannes Schneider's influence, brought all schools and instructors into the Arlberg technique.

The all-steel cable binding came along in 1933, sparking more interest in racing. Racing was the *raison d'être* for establishing the *Fédération Internationale de Ski* (FIS) in 1924. In the 1937 races under the auspices of the FIS, Emile Allais caught the attention of the skiing world with his parallel technique.

During World War II years, 1939-1946, European ski instruction was largely confined to the training of mountain troops for combat and transportation.

Then, as skiing revived after the war, Austrian

Anton Seelos, who coached the French racing team in the 1948 Winter Olympics, scored major victories with two men, Couttet and Oreiller, using a new-style relaxed technique that permitted quicker action in executing turns. Soon all the world's skiers were using the younger European's hip and leg action instead of rotation. Shoulders were held still, creating a reversed-shoulder appearance. About this time, Swiss skiers began to stress sideslipping and greater movement of hips, legs and ankles to achieve greater turning power.

By 1954, Austrian experts were analyzing the techniques of the best racers in the FIS. They came up with the "comma" position, emphasizing hip and leg action and eliminating rotation completely.

In the U.S., the National Ski Association fielded a demonstration team in 1959 at a national ski school meeting. This team showed a remarkable similarity of technique, inspiring instructors all over the country to cooperate in developing a purely American technique. This was published in 1964 by the Professional Ski Instructors of America (PSIA) as *The Official American Ski Technique*.

Modern skiing has advanced through the individual efforts of men and women who have promoted the sport—teaching, building ski areas, organizing clubs and fostering competition. The film industry has done much to glamorize the sport. Promotion programs of winter sports resorts have stimulated the growth of uphill lifts and facilities.

Skiing will continue to grow and change in technique as a result of technology and research. Teaching methods and teaching techniques will continue to evolve as a result of improved communication among instructors. Development of improved skiing techniques through the PSIA is evidence of this continuing growth in the U.S. Today we see techniques and styles merging, so that differences are visually less obvious.

Success in competitive skiing, which has led to nationalism and commercialism of skiing techniques, will probably continue to be influential. Contemporary ski techniques are the result of evolution and technological progress. The sharing of ideas among nations has brought better understanding and appreciation of diverse techniques. The professional ski instructors of the United States have developed confidence in their own concepts. They have been able to recognize the best elements of other techniques and are intent on maintaining an up-to-date and natural system of ski instruction.

Non-profit ski organizations have played a major role in the development of the sport.

The daddy of them all is the United States Ski Association, (USSA) founded in 1904 by Merritt Stiles. The USSA has seven divisions, including Hawaii and Alaska. It was originally known as the National Ski Association; the name was changed in 1962.

Membership in the USSA offers many advantages—standardized level of competent instruction, sponsorship of local ski meets, support of the U.S. Olympic teams, representation in other world class events, support of the National Youth Ski Program and safety programs, publication of booklets and proficiency tests.

The affiliated associations are listed by area: Central U.S., Far West, Pacific Northwest, Northern Rocky Mountain, Rocky Mountain, and Southern Rocky Mountain; U.S. Eastern Amateur Ski Association.

These seven local offices coordinate ski programs and function year-round for skiers' benefit. The only paid employee in most offices is the executive secretary; all the other officers are volunteers. They are informational clearing houses for everybody—the individual skier, the instructor, the ski patrolman, the lift operator, governmental agencies and the ski industry.

Members and representatives meet regularly with their area councils and through annual conventions and Fall Forums, render service to the membership through newsletters and other communication.

The National Ski Patrol System (NSPS) is made up partly of volunteers, partly of paid personnel. These men and women provide rescue and first aid treatment for injured skiers throughout the U.S. and the NSPS European division. Members are divided into registered classifications: Auxiliary Member, Junior Ski Patrolman, Certified Ski Patrolman, National Ski Patrolman, and Retired Member. Members register with the NSPS through their area councils. Registered ski patrols are organized into sections, regions and divisions.

In addition to rescue and first aid, the NSPS promotes safety and accident prevention in cooperation with ski area management, ski instructors, the United States Ski Association, the U.S. Forest Service, the

National Park Service, the military, the American Red Cross and the local State Highway Patrol.

Each division has an instructors' association whose main purpose is to improve and to standardized instruction methods. They protect the public from incompetent instruction, protect the professional instructor from unfair competition, encourage skiers to take lessons, and generally promote competence and professionalism. These purposes are backed by the Professional Ski Instructors of America, (PSIA) the parent organization of certified ski instructors.

Chapter 2

CONDITIONING

Ski authorities agree that the entire body should be in good physical condition before attempting to learn skiing or before returning to the slopes after the off-season. Good physical condition can be developed by continued participation in any vigorous running sport and swimming. However, a progressive physical conditioning program of selected exercises designed to increase strength, flexibility, coordination and endurance is also recommended.

For the non-competitive recreational skier, two or more months should be spent on conditioning. A typical daily ski fitness program should be ten weeks in length, consisting of one-half hour calisthenics covering 16 exercises, some involving rotational movements of the body, increasing to 40 minutes; men should run three-quarters of a mile, increasing to 1½ miles; women should run a quarter of a mile, increasing to 1 mile; all should participate in tumbling and gymnastic work on the horse, parallel bars, and trampoline.

We have outlined a program of weight-lifting which develops strength through the specific adaptation of the body to imposed demands. This is the "overload principle." The overloading is carried on by a progressive, gradual increase in the weights used, thereby assuring a continuity of strength gains in desired body areas. Although there are many sports that develop strength in the legs and ankles, there is no occupational activity or sport that will develop a high level of strength in the musculature surrounding the knee joint. Klein and Hall, in their intensive studies of athletic knee injuries, found that the higher the level of strength developed in the muscles surrounding the knee through preconditioning drills and progressive resistence exercises (leg extension and leg curl), the lower the risk of injury.

The prospective recreational skier seldom gives attention to developing strength and flexibility in the lower back muscles. Yet this is the most vulnerable part of the body, from the standpoint of muscular strains, in or out of the sports world. Baumgartner* comments that lumbago and sciatic pain occur frequently, particularly in older and overweight skiers. There is a tendency not to report this type of strain as a ski injury.

Some advocates of weight training recommend that a fitness program should cover a minimum period of four months. A program of progressive weight training should supplement a physical education class in skiing. Weight lifting should be performed two or three days a week outside of the physical education class, hours to be arranged by the student. During the ski class, students should perform conditioning exercises designed to increase strength, cardio-respiratory endurance and flexibility. Running should be done during the physical education class or on the days between weight lifting.

WARM-UP AND CONDITIONING EXERCISES

Here are some exercises that can be performed at home with no equipment. It is recommended that at least a half-hour of vigorous warm-ups precede skills practice and instruction in a dry-land ski class. Flexibility exercises and stretching should both precede and follow more vigorous movement.

Phantom chair Lean against a wall with back flat,

Phantom chair

*Baumgartner, W., "Skiing and the Vertebral Column," Abstracts of Foreign Physical Education Literature, Indianapolis: Phi Epsilon Kappa, Vol. 8, 1963.

thighs at right angles to the lower leg; gradually increase time held. Heels may be raised to increase difficulty. This increases strength in the quadriceps and gastrocnemius.

Trunk raising

Trunk raising and bending From a prone position, with hands clasped behind back, feet held down, raise chest from the floor; rotate upper body to the left as far as possible and hold for five seconds; return to starting position; repeat right 10 times; increase repetitions gradually. Increases strength of extensors of the spine.

Pushups Women may do a modified pushup with body in a straight line from knee to the shoulder; men keep entire body straight, lower to within one inch of floor.

Situps Use a bent knee position with feet secured or held down. Hands behind head, pull up and twist elbow to opposite knee.

Flutter kick Sit or lie on one side, swing straight legs so one knee passes the other, as in a flutter kick. Increases strength of abdominals and hip flexors.

Flutter kick

Woodchopper

Sit and stand With skis secured to the boots, sit on back of the skis then rise to a standing position, throwing arms forward from overhead; repeat; increase repetitions gradually. Increases strength of the abdominals and quadriceps.

Woodchopper Legs apart, swing arms far back between legs, bending knees, return to arms overhead; repeat, gradually increase repetitions.

Burpees (squat-thrusts) Four counts—place hands on floor, bending knees, count one; jump legs to full extension backwards, count two; jump back to the position of count one, count three; stand, count four; repeat. A six-count burpee may be used for triceps strength by adding a pushup. Increases strength in the quadriceps, triceps, gluteals, and back.

Running in place Lift feet high (eight inches from floor) while running in place; increase time of the exercise gradually. Increase to 12 minutes. Improves cardio-respiratory endurance and leg strength.

Squat-jump Hands on top of head—feet placed one behind the other; jump eight to 10 inches from a half knee bend, landing with feet reversed; keep the trunk upright.

Pillow-jump Jump from side to side with feet together and arms out to the side for balance over a pillow or imaginary object. Try for a jump of a foot or more.

When performing exercises which stretch muscles beyond the normal range of movement, the stretch reflex is automatically activated. This stretch reflex is a protective mechanism of the body which prevents muscles from tearing; the muscle to be stretched actually contracts to protect itself and the result is pain.

To avoid excessive muscle soreness which usually accompanies ballistic stretches, use only static stretches. Simply stretch to the maximum, just to the point of resistance, holding and relaxing totally with the body's weight maintaining the stretch.

In skiing we are primarily interested in increasing flexibility in the backs of the legs, the hamstrings and the Achilles tendons. Here are some examples of static stretches which should precede and follow a workout and running:

Crossed-leg stretch Standing, cross the right leg over the left, place left hand on right shoulder, lower left elbow toward floor to your maximum stretch with straight legs. Hold the position for 10 to 15 counts. Return slowly to standing and repeat on the opposite side.

Forward-lunge stretch Standing as in a lunge, back leg straight, forward leg bent, forward foot turned out for balance and the back foot straight forward to effect the stretch, press forward, lowering the body deeper into the lunge to your maximum stretch. Hold for 10 to 15 counts. Repeat opposite.

Sideward-lunge stretch Standing, lunge sideward to the right, keeping the left leg straight and left foot directed forward. Hold at your maximum stretch 10 to 15 counts. Repeat opposite.

Stride-sit stretch Sit with legs in a wide "V" position, knees directed upward. 'Round" the back, lowering the chest toward the left, center and right, holding at maximum stretch at each position for 10 to 15 counts.

Lower back stretch Sitting, knees bent, bottoms of feet together, "round" forward to maximum stretch. Hold 10 to 15 counts.

Hurdle stretch Sitting with right leg straight, left leg bent with left knee on the floor, legs at right angles, lower chest toward knee and floor. Hold at maximum for 10 to 15 counts. Repeat opposite.

Straight-leg stretch Sitting, legs straight in front, reach forward toward toes. If your flexibility permits, grasp toes and hold at maximum stretch for 10 to 15 counts.

Quadriceps stretch Standing, bend left knee and grasp the left ankle behind with the left hand, pressing heel toward the buttocks. Hold at maximum stretch. Repeat opposite. The exercise may be executed on the floor by kneeling, grasping both ankles and leaning backward.

PROGRESSIVE WEIGHT TRAINING

The "double progressive" system of weight training is used, providing regular increases in the amount of weight and repetitions. Eight to 10 repetitions are recommended for the upper body starting with eight repetitions; add one repetition each workout period until a total of 10 repetitions is reached. Then add the suggested weight increase starting over at eight repetitions. Twenty to 40 repetitions are recommended for waist and legs.

On exercises where an increase in strength is desired, use the set system, three sets (repeating the desired number of lifts three times, resting between each set). In exercises where a loss of weight is desired or when increasing endurance, do all the repetitions in one set, using a light weight.

Progressive overloading of the muscles is required for strength increases. Whatever weight is used, the exerciser must strain to complete the final one or two repetitions. If completed with ease, the weight is not heavy enough.

If it is necessary to strain on the final one or two repetitions so the exercise cannot be performed correctly, the weight is too heavy. Exercises should be done at a moderate pace. When using light weights to reduce or increase endurance, work fast.

Strength training periods cover approximately 45 minutes, providing three-minute rest periods between exercises and two-minute rest periods between sets. As physical condition improves, the length of rest periods can be reduced. A workout should be completed every other day or three days a week, e.g.: Monday, Wednesday, Friday omiting Saturday and Sunday.

During the second workout, add five, 10, 15 pounds for each exercise and do required repetitions. During third and fourth sessions, add weight again. At some period during the first four sessions, it will be found the required repetitions cannot be completed as the weight is too heavy. Reduce weight accordingly (five, 10 or 15 pounds). This weight will then be the program starting poundage to which weight increases will be added on a weekly basis.

Curls (On Universal Gym Machine or with barbell) Stand erect, barbell at hang position in front of thighs. Bend elbows raising weight to chest; then lower barbell.

Arm curls

Bench press   Lie on bench, hands slightly wider than shoulder-width apart; press weight to arms length; lower and repeat.

Dips or triceps extension   Use parallel bars, barbells, or Universal Gym Machine.

Rowing   (with barbell) Body bent at 90° angle to floor, back straight, head up, knees slightly bent; weight hanging free approximately three inches from ground, hands slightly wider than shoulder-width apart; raise weight to lower chest, elbows facing outward; lower to arms length without touching floor and repeat. (May be performed on a Universal Gym Machine.)

High leg press   (On Universal Gym Machine) Place feet on the higher position, press to full extension, lower without banging the weight.

Dips

Situps   Lie on floor, knees in bent knee position, feet secured, weight behind neck; curl trunk forward to sit, lower and repeat; most persons will have to start without weights. Progression can be: (1) arms folded on chest, (2) hands behind neck, (3) small barbell, (4) feet elevated on a slant board. If situps tend to strain your lower back use Leg Overs. Leg Overs: arms straight holding handle of incline bench, tuck knees, extend legs and touch wall behind head, lower legs and extend, repeat.

Toe raise   Place toes on two- to four-inch block of wood. Feet eight to 10 inches apart; toes pointed inward on first two sets; straight ahead on the third; raise as high as possible on toes; lower and attempt to touch heels to floor; hold to count of two in lower position to stretch lower calves.

Leg extension   Completely straighten legs on upswing so knees lock; lower weights and repeat. The last one-half inch on the extension is the most important; lift slowly.

Leg curl   Lie face down on bench; raise lower legs until heels touch buttocks; completely straighten legs when weight is lowered.

Toe raises

Rope jump This exercise is started after four weeks on first nine exercises. Tie rope to two chairs, 16 to 18 inches from floor with a little slack in rope. Stand erect facing rope with dumbbells in hands at sides; jump over rope; raising knees as high as possible and swinging dumbbells forwards and upwards. Stand sideways to rope facing in same direction; jump sideways over rope, repeat from opposite side five times. After two weeks stand with back to rope, jump backward over rope flexing knees and raising them as high as possible.

There are several supplementary activities which can be recommended to the student. These are selected because of their effectiveness in developing leg strength, and cardio-respiratory endurance (in order of effectiveness): running up and down stairs, hilly terrain, dry sand at the beach, a dry land slalom, or jumping through a series of tires; jumping rope; basic trampoline skills; soccer or tennis; bicycling; jumping and hopping up steps.

The following instructional aids may be used to simulate skiing action and/or to develop balance, coordination or timing. These might be used as a challenge along with dodging games and dryland slalom running exercises.

Bongo Board Improves balance, coordination and leg strength. The Bongo Board comes in two pieces— a roller which has a square groove and the board with a track along the bottom that fits in the groove. The skier stands on the board with weight evenly distributed on both feet. The object is to stay in balance while rolling the board from side to side.

Ski Way Simulates the feeling of angulation and develops leg strength and coordination. It consists of parallel bars, elevated from the floor in the center in the form of an arc. A platform which supports the skier moves over the tubular bars on ball-bearing nylon wheels. Elastic straps under the platform are attached to either end of the device to pull the platform back across the bars. An additional attachment has been devised to permit edge control.

Chapter 3

SKIS

Selection of skis must be made with consideration of the individual skier's ability, height and weight, budget and personal preference. However, before these details are determined, some knowledge of the basics of ski design must be understood.

The most important functions of the ski are its ability to: track, dge and turn. Tracking refers to the ability of the ski to hold a straight line when pressure is released from the inside edge of the tip of the ski. Ability to edge means the ski tail follows directly in the groove or trail of the tip without skidding or slipping sideways. Ability to turn means the ski will describe an arc on the snow as a result of the arc which is built into the side of the ski.

The beginning skier should look for a ski which has an even flex throughout its entire length. Check the flex by placing the heel of ski against the right instep, holding the tip in the left hand. Push downward with the right hand in the ski center. For hard-packed snow an advanced skier will want the ski to increase in firmness past center flex toward the tail.

Flex patterns vary in different models according to the use for which the ski was designed. The giant slalom (GS) has an even flex while a slalom (SL) ski has a stiff tail and flexible tip. With skiers tending to ski more on the tails, pushing the tips ahead, a tip is required that will conform to the contour of the terrain.

Downhill models are slightly wider and are best designed for high speed. Their flex is stiff in the tail and flexible in the tip.

When the bottoms of skis are placed together, you will notice a curve from tip to tail. This curve, called bottom camber, distributes the skier's weight evenly along the running surface. Unless a skier is able to easily pinch his skies closed with two fingers and a thumb, his skis are too stiff. The space provided by bottom camber should be three-quarters to one-and-one-quarter inch for the recreational skier.

Side camber (side cut) means the sides are curved. In other words, the width of the ski differs from tip to tail: widest at the tip, narrower at the tail and narrowest at the center. Side camber causes the edges of the skis to skid slightly when moving straight forward. Side camber also promotes turning. When the ski turns sharply, it skids, flexes and torques slightly. Torque refers to the ski's ability to conform longitudinally to the irregularities of the slope. Therefore, side camber, flexibility and torsion are built into the ski to aid in its turning ability. Side camber is identical for the GS and SL skis.

All skis are designed with the same general physical characteristics. Tips turn up to allow the skis to move over uneven terrain without diving into the snow. Tips help prevent skis from crossing. Bottoms are smooth and flush with steel edges except for a longitudinal groove necessary for tracking ability. Edges may be of one piece or of short interlocking steel segments. They are sharp and may extend slightly beyond the ski's sides. Thickness changes from a thick center to a thinner tip and tail.

The recent successes of ski manufacturers with combinations of plastics and wood, along with various attempts in pure metal and pure plastic construction, have led to a domination by the epoxy ski. The original solid hickory or laminated wood ski is an antique. The metal-wood combination ski is definitely losing popularity.

A metal ski is made of two thin metal sheets or

skins bonded to and separated by a wood core. The metal ski reacts instantaneously to the slightest impulse. The result is that sideslipping and skidding are made easy. Metal skis do not torque well: the less torque, the less chance of hooking or hanging up edges. Some racers find them desirable for high-speed downhill competition.

Plastic skis, under varied names are the most popular at the moment. The basic material is fiber glass-reinforced laminated sheets of polyester or epoxy resins. The material is produced from millions of tiny glass fibers which are first made into threads. These are woven into a loose cloth which is then dipped into resin which cures under heat and pressure into a hard, glass-like material. Density and resiliency can be varied by varying the pressure under which it is cured.

A good-quality plastic ski will perform with some of the best characteristics of both wood and metal skis. They track beautifully, are generally easy to turn, and hold well on ice. A combination of materials is also used: metal with wood core and reinforcing sheets of fiber glass. A pure fiber glass ski is completely encased in glass while some have an outer layer of fiber glass only.

When selecting a ski, you should consider that the ski, if properly selected, will perform well at speeds up to 15 m.p.h. which is the most popular recreational speed. The average skier is not bold enough to ski at higher speeds and therefore is unable to use the help of centrifugal force in turning. As speed increases, friction decreases and skis become easy to turn. However, modern terrain requires that you slow down on steep slopes and bumpy runs. Therefore, the ideal ski would be one that would turn easily at slow speeds and would also offer stability and security at higher speeds.

It might be said that selecting a ski is like buying shoes. Once you decide on the price level or brand name, you must decide on size. This refers not only to length but to the flex of the skis as related to body weight and strength. All skis vary with regard to flex. Wood varies in density, metals vary due to temperature changes. The greatest variant is the skier himself, with his differences in height, weight, strength and ability.

Step one is to decide on the length of the skis. Length and speed are relative. In other words, the faster you go the more wheelbase you need. If you are a beginner, you should select a ski approximately your height or shorter. This is because you will be skiing at slow speeds, almost steering your turns rather than skidding them (approximately five to seven m.p.h.)

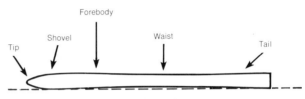

Ski from above, showing side camber

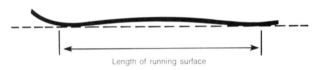

Ski from side, showing bottom camber

The magic length, recommended today by the Professional Ski Instructors of America, is 150 centimeters—shorter for children and small adults. As the student progresses to basic christies, he can progress to 170 centimeter skis. The next progression would be to 180 centimeters. Thereafter, the length depends on the individual's personal preference. Even advanced students are discovering the benefit of shorter lengths for learning complicated maneuvers. The graduated length method (GLM) is being taught at most schools.

Step two, a most important step, is to select the proper flex for your weight. A ski, placed on a table base down, will touch only at tip and tail. The ski should rise in the middle about three-eighths- to one-half inch. Bottom camber is a curvature, designed to control weight distribution on the ski. Now add soft or semi-soft snow beneath the ski with a 175-pound skier on top, pushing down, and the ski will bend into an opposite curve or reverse camber. It is this arc which is most important in making a ski turn. If your weight is sufficient to make a ski bend into a three-inch arc, you will ski effortlessly. However, if you are too light, you will produce only a straight edge, which will cause trouble. It will be difficult to initiate a turn. A third possibility is one in which the skis are too soft for the skier. This skier may cross his skis in front, or even the tails. His tracks will look like a series of linked recoveries.

When you ski on a ski of the proper tension, you feel as if you were skiing only on the tail of the ski and the forebody is merely a feeler. The reverse is all too apparent. If the ski is too stiff, all you will feel is a mile of ski out in front of you. As an advanced skier, you will experience the curved turn as if it were happening under the arch of your foot. It will follow the curve of your arch as if the edge were on your foot, rather than on the ski.

If you consider your ski as a whole, most of the weight, or the heaviest part, will be under your foot with little pressure on tip or tail. As the speed increases, so does the pressure on the whole ski, tip to tail, giving added holding power from the skis' edges.

But, as speed decreases, so does the pressure, almost as if your ski becomes shorter at slower speeds and longer as speed goes up. This is possibly because of the high elasticity of fiber glass and its uncanny ability to bend out of shape and to return quickly without staying bent.

The action of the modern ski in varying terrain may be compared to butter flowing down the slope, conforming to the humps and gullies. Since you have more of the ski edge on the snow you can use a softer ski. The ski of yesterday did not conform as well. It had to be stiffer since a smaller portion was in contact with the snow. If all slopes were flat and uniform this would not be a problem.

POLES

The variety of ski poles available for selection is confusing even for the experienced skier. However, here are a few important points to look for:

Manipulation The feel of the pole as it is manipulated in a flicking action will be a determining factor. More weight near the handle will permit easier and quicker manipulation than if the weight is concentrated near the basket, therefore the pole must be tapered. This affords strength as well as balance.

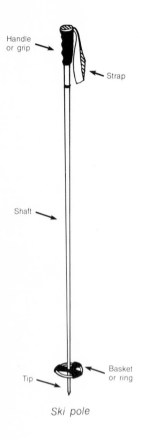

Handle or grip

Strap

Shaft

Basket or ring

Tip

Ski pole

Shaft The shaft may be made of steel, steel alloys, aluminum, fiber glass or bamboo. Inclusion of nickel with other metals will increase resiliency. The lighter weight of the fiber glass and aluminum poles is the reason for their popularity. Aluminum is vulnerable to cuts from ski edges which could weaken the pole and cause it to bend. Steel is stronger but lacks resiliency; under extreme force, steel poles will snap. Since "hot-dogging" and more vigorous turns have become popular, some pole manufacturers have attempted to alleviate shock by devising spring loaded anti-shock devices built into the shaft of the pole.

Some models have a bend in the shaft just below the grip which allows the skier to reach out for his pole-plants more easily. One of the newest innovations is a pole in three sections joined by an interlocking system. Replacement sections are available. Manufacturers are trying to attract interest by updating their products with a "mod" look. Anodized colors are permanent and are coordinated with ski colors. Wild geometric designs decorate the shafts. Another design has a different attraction, the drink pole. It has a hidden compartment in the handle for liquid refreshment.

Handles The most comfortable and the most durable handles are molded plastic, contoured to fit the grip. Some grips have a contoured platform on which the hand rests providing support for performing gymnastic maneuvers.

Wrist straps Wrist straps are usually adjustable and should fit the wrist to permit a solid grip while wearing ski gloves or mittens. As a safety factor, some wrist straps will release with a given force.

Rings The ring, about three inches from the bottom of the pole, is made of a hard rubber, aluminum or plastic.

Tips A moderately sharp point at the tip is necessary for penetrating hard snow or ice. Competition models may have a tip which is an ice prong on a tungsten carbide point. Another device for safety is a pole with a retractable spring-loaded tip. The tip comes out of the shaft only when pressure is applied.

Length The proper length of the ski pole depends upon your height. Hold the pole, handle resting on the floor, and grasp under the basket. If the pole is the correct length for you, the forearm should be parallel to the floor. Poles can be cut down to the proper size. Any ski shop will do this for a small charge.

BINDINGS

Selection should be based on the skier's weight, strength and skiing ability. The ski shop operators are experts in mounting bindings and will recommend top quality merchandise within the skier's budget and for the individual's needs. There are several types of bindings. Only a binding which has releasing action adjusted to the individual's ability and weight should be used. The "bear trap," a toe-piece and cable which does not release the boot in a fall, is unsafe and is no longer used. Cable bindings are also obsolete, although occasionally they are seen in rentals.

All the popular bindings have at least three basic angles of release—laterally (left and right) at the toe and upwards at the heel. The argument against an upward release at the toe or a lateral release at the heel is that this complicates adjustment. However, some manufacturers do offer these additional releases and contend that it is possible to arrive at a ratio of upward to sideward release at both toe and heel that is safe.

Some features to look for are: (1) ease of adjustment and repair, (2) inability of the adjustment to jiggle loose, (3) moving parts which are not exposed and likely to ice up, (4) compactness, minimum hardware, and 5) immovable bond of the boot during normal maneuvers.

The binding is only as safe as the skier who uses it. Without proper adjustment, the binding is ineffective. Your local ski shop has the equipment for adjusting your bindings to your ski ability and weight. Safety straps should always be used to keep a released ski from running downhill and possibly injuring another skier. Safety straps may be made of leather or nylon, and either wrap around the boot or simply clip to the boot.

Friction plates under the boot are being used to facilitate releases. Adjustments of the bindings and these friction release plates (FRP) should be checked each time the skis are used if chances of malfunction are to be reduced. Never tighten down your bindings yourself or allow someone on the hill to change the adjustment. Go to the area repair shop for help!

BOOTS

Everyone in the skiing business will agree that the most important piece of skiing equipment is the boot. Transmittal of body movement to the skis is only possible if the boot holds the foot firmly without allowing slipping, lifting, or twisting. Ankle flexion is permitted but lateral ankle movement is necessarily restricted. The toes must have ample room so that circulation is not restricted, but the heel should be held quite firmly in place.

The buckle boot has replaced the laced type because of its popularity. A primary selling point of the buckle boot over the lace boot is the speed of putting it on with the advantages of loosening the buckles between runs.

The ski boot salesman in a reliable ski shop is usually well-trained in procedures for fitting and adjusting the boot. He will instruct the purchaser in proper methods of buckling or lacing ond his suggestions should be followed.

Another choice has to be made by the skier, among leather, plastics, or a composite. The trend in boot materials is definitely toward plastics in boot construction. Plastic boots can be produced inexpensively, once the molds are designed. Some other advantages are that no damage can be caused by water or flexion, plastic is extremely durable, little or no maintenance is required, and the foaming or self-molding materials within the inner boot can give a custom fit.

Some disadvantages are that they do not conform to the foot at normal temperatures (however, when heated, the shape can be altered to relieve pressure spots); they have a memory and tend to return to their original shape; the feet can become damp from perspiration and condensation since plastic is non-absorbent; engineering and new molds for new models can be very expensive; and "foamed-to-fit boots" cannot be resold unless the liner can be replaced or the plastic can be removed.

WAX AND WAXING TECHNIQUES

Most skis today have an adequate factory base. However, the new base is somewhat porous and should be sealed by a hot wax method, by a liquid base lacquer, or both.

Some snow conditions will require the use of rubbed-on wax. The purpose of the wax is to eliminate the drag or resistance that certain snow conditions create. Waxes are especially necessary in racing and ski jumping to eliminate hydro-adhesion (a type of suction). Also, at certain temperatures, snow will stick to the ski bottoms, acting as brake. Even with wax, this icing up will occur when warm skis are placed on the snow before they have adjusted to the air temperature. Place the skis in an outdoor rack for about 15 minutes before using and this problem can be eliminated.

No two skiers will agree on the kind of wax to use under every condition, but here are a few basic suggestions. A wax kit should include at least three kinds of wax: two for the two extremes in temperatures and one average wax for normal snow conditions.

If you were to wax your skis accurately for the ultimate in speed, you would be waxing for every five degrees of change in temperature. Therefore, the general rule is: the colder the snow, the harder the wax.

Waxes are identified by color or number; for instance, green and blue are hard waxes, while red and silver are softer waxes (see Elementary Waxing Chart). Ordinary kitchen paraffin is a good soft wax.

ELEMENTARY WAXING CHART

Air Temp.	Snow Moisture and Texture	Color of Container
32°F and above	{ Very slushy Corn	Silver (softer wax)
32°F	Moist	Red (softer wax)
18°F	{ Dry Very dry	Blue (harder wax)
10°F	Extremely dry	Green (harder wax)

Note: Use Gold as a base coat under the above waxes. Use Red as a sealer on all new skis.

F	41	32	23	14	5	0	-4	-13	-22
C	5	0	-5	-10	-15	-17.8	-20	-25	-30

(To convert fahrenheit to centigrade, subtract 32 and multiply by 5/9.)

(To convert centigrade to fahrenheit, multiply by 9/5 and add 32.)

In warmer weather the need for wax becomes greater as the snow gets wetter. However, on some types of cold snow, the base lacquer or factory base is all that is necessary. Waxes made in Europe will use centigrade in the packaged instructions, so a conversion table is included here.

Spring skiing enthusiasts will attest to the effectiveness of using melted wax or combinations of waxes applied with a paint brush. Melted paraffin and moth balls makes an excellent base. Starting at the tail and working to the tip, brush so that the strokes are overlapping. This overlapping causes an uneven build-up of wax which will create an air flow between the ski and the snow, thus allowing a faster running surface. This type of waxing is effective when the snow becomes very wet and sticky.

The beginning skier may not be too interested in making his skis any faster than they are, until he understands that the smoother they glide over the surface of the snow, the easier they are to turn (less friction). Also, changeable snow is easier to ski when skis are properly waxed.

CLOTHING

Choices are often made in terms of fashion dictates. If looking "right" can give the novice added confidence, he should make every effort toward this advantage.

Clothing must be selected in terms of warmth, comfort and durability. Layers of highly insulated clothing which trap body heat will keep you warm. Lightweight materials are preferable to heavy bulky types.

Fuzzy, longhaired fabrics or knits are impractical. Cotton is the best material next to the skin; outer layers should be windproof and water repellant. Water repellant does not mean waterproof. Water repellancy wears off, but can be restored with one of several aerosol products. The fit should be snug but not tight since a flow of trapped body heat must be permitted within these layers of clothing.

Closely fitted clothing at the neck, wrists and waist will reduce heat loss. Check tags for cleaning and washing instructions. Ask about shrinkage, especially in turtleneck shirts. Zippers will work better if you rub paraffin or candle wax over teeth. Watch out for heat from fireplaces, cigarettes, extreme heat from irons or room heaters. Dry gloves and boots away from heaters. Cotton is inflammable, wool chars, synthetics melt. Some cuts or rips from skis, poles, rocks, ski lifts are unavoidable. Novices should choose durable fabrics.

Underwear Tops with long sleeves and long bottoms can be had in a bonded two-layer fabric of cotton inside and wool outside. Fish-net underwear traps body heat in the holes and is very warm when worn next to the skin. In very hot weather, this same fish-net shirt has a cooling effect when worn as a sole garment.

Socks Socks are made in wool or wool-nylon combination; some varieties, called thermo socks, provide a cushioned springy weave on the inside. Some skiers prefer two pair of socks; a very light pair of cotton next to the skin and the outer of wool. With molded boots, the trend is toward one thin pair. Color is unimportant since the socks are worn *under the ski pants*.

Turtleneck shirts Turtleneck shirts are made of cotton or synthetics such as orlon, nylon, or banlon. Cotton is more absorbent than synthetics. Watch out for necks that stretch out of shape. Some brands are not guaranteed against shrinkage.

Ski pants Pants usually are made of a stretch fabric. This fabric combines a stretchable nylon or spandex fiber with wool or with a synthetic such as rayon or acrylic. The price range is very great; the price of a sturdy, lightly woven *wool-nylon* or *wool-spandex* is well worth the money. Stretch pants are meant to be fitted snugly; be sure not to buy them too long. Be sure the crotch does not hang low or seams may split.

Ski sweaters Sweaters are available in many styles and colors. Select a smooth hard finish yarn, not a soft fuzzy yarn. One fall in the snow will show why.

Parkas This lightweight jacket is well insulated due to its three layers: lining, insulated filler and wind-water proof outer fabric. A hood, which is neatly tucked out of sight in a zippered compartment at the neck, is recommended in case the temperature drops or the wind comes up while you are on the slopes. For very cold or windy weather, a down-filled parka is extremely desirable. Lightweight and warm even without a sweater, they are well worth the extra cost. Extremely light weight are the synthetic foam-lined parkas, almost as warm as down.

Warmup pants Usually made of the same materials as the parkas, they sometimes are made of denim. They are worn over the ski pants in very cold weather and can be had with a matching parka. Some designs are one-piece jumpsuits or overalls. Some warmup pants are tailored to fit tighter and are worn in lieu of ski pants.

Gloves or mittens Made of leather of soft or rough durable quality, they are usually lined with a soft cotton flannel or a furlike insulation. Mittens are much warmer than gloves of an equal weight. There is less area through which heat may be lost because fingers are not separated. The warmest mittens are filled with down.

However, gloves are less bulky and are preferred by more experienced skiers. A fine silk glove worn as a liner under gloves, or even under mittens in extremely cold weather is very effective for added protection.

Head gear Head coverings can run the gamut from an ear-protecting headband to real fur. Avoid any dangling gear or long hair that could catch in lift mechanisms.

Goggles and sunglasses Skiers should have more than one pair of both in case one pair is lost or damaged. The eyes must be protected *at all times*. Whether the sun is bright or the sky is overcast, the eyes can be burned or irritated because of wind and/or extreme light reflection from the snow. Some goggles and sunglasses have removable lenses. Yellow lenses are used when skies are overcast or when skiing in shaded areas. Clear lenses may be used in a snowstorm. Darker lenses are necessary for bright sunlight.

Goggles are used primarily for snowy or wintry days. The most recent innovation is goggles or sunglasses which have lenses adaptable to both shade and bright sunlight. Some are guaranteed against fogging inside from your body warmth or breath. Some de-fogging products are available for coating the inside of the lens. One's own saliva works fairly well. All goggles must be well vented at the sides, but if vented at the top, snow will fall into the eyelashes.

After-ski boots   After-ski boots might be considered a non-essential extra, but they are necessary in some instances. If the skier must walk any distance in the snow, ski boots should not be worn, and ordinary footwear will slip dangerously. An after-ski boot should rise high enough above the ankle to prevent snow from entering, and should have a well-cut tread.

CHECK LIST FOR PACKING

The following check list of clothing and accessories will be a handy reminder before each ski trip. You will want to add to this list and keep it stored with ski gear for efficient packing.

Boots	Goggles, lenses
Skis	Sunglasses
Poles	Suntan lotion
Gloves and liners	and sun screen
Mittens	Lip cream
Headgear	Cosmetics
Long johns	Shaving kit
Turtleneck shirts	Anti-freeze
Socks, heavy, light	Flashlight
Sweaters	Tow chain
Parka	Shovel
Ski pants	Sand
Warmup pants	Powdered bleach
After-ski clothes	Car ski rack
After-ski boots	Extra car keys
Filing kit	Flares
Ski wax	Camera, film
First aid kit	Battery jumper cable
Matches	Money, checks
Alarm clock	Credit cards
Chains	

CARE OF SKIS

Check for concaveness or convexness and railed or rounded edges. Metal skis require little or no care except for maintaining sharp edges. This job is best done at a ski shop where they are equipped for this purpose, but a specially designed file may be purchased. Hand sharpening of wood or epoxy skis can be done with a good ten-inch No. 15 mill bastard file. It isn't necessary to have a vise but it does make the job easier.

Place the ski in a vise with the edge up and the running surface of the ski away from you. The file should be drawn diagonally across the steel edge, working from tip to tail, cutting only on the forward stroke. Be careful to keep the file level. While working, wipe the skis free of filings with an oiled cloth every few strokes. The file should be kept clean with a wire file brush. Next, remove skis from vise and flat-file the bottoms lightly from tail to tip. Keep heels of hands on the running surface to prevent the file from tilting.

Old skis may have a convex base, railed edges or rounded edges. Be aware of these conditions before you buy.

New skis should be flat filed before they leave the ski shop. Contrary to popular belief, most new skis, no matter what quality, are not properly filed ready for use. The edges tend to have a slight concavity which will cause hooking or hanging of outside edges.

The edges on approximately the first eight inches of running surface at the tip and tail should be dulled by running a quarter or file over this area. If this area is overly sharp, the skis will tend to hook or turn into the hill (referred to as 'edgy').

Railed edges   Convex   Concave   Flat

Bottom configurations of skis

According to United States Olympic Gold Medalist Billy Kidd, skis have been traditionally designed with concave running surfaces in order to track well and hold on ice. Today's modern ski structure is sufficiently effective so that Billy prefers a convex bottom, which makes starting a turn and changing edges much easier,

With slightly rounded bottoms, he feels he can use longer, more stable skis that will also turn quickly (e.g.: a 220 cm ski with a convex bottom is equal in turning ease to a 210 cm ski with a concave running surface). For a convex base, Billy's filing system is quite different from the flat filing described earlier. (See *Ski Magazine,* Holiday issue, 1970).

Billy places the ski against a wall and stabilizes it with his knees. Starting from the mid-section, he works up the left side to the tip and then down the right side. To file the tail section, he turns the ski upside down and places the tail against the wall.

The file handle must be intentionally lifted slightly to remove more base material near the edge in order to give the desired convex base. Position the file so that the grooves in the file run parallel to the ski's polyethylene base. To file from tip to tail on the right side, the file is turned over so the handle is on the left side of the skis, keeping the grooves running parallel with the edge. The amount of overhang of the file must be consistent in order that the lines on the edges caused by the file may be straight. Pressure on the downward stroke, releasing to a light feathering on the release will prevent any diagonal cuts.

To file the sides, place the tip in a corner of the room with the bottom facing left; hold the tail in the left hand and with the right hand file from within eight inches of the tail toward the tip. Holding the ski between the knees, file toward the mid section of the ski; hold the file at a 90 degree angle to the bottom of the ski and maintain an equal overhang of the file.

At the binding, turn the file lengthwise on the edge with the handle toward you, push along the edge with the left hand, keeping the file flat with the right. To finish the tip, place the ski against the wall and file from the waist to the tip, holding the ski between the knees. File the opposite edge by placing the tail in the corner with the base facing left and repeat the steps just described.

Once a year, it would be advisable to have a reliable ski shop repair any damage to the base and prepare the edges to your specifications. For the rest of the season, take care of the edges yourself with a light dressing of the edges at the end of every ski day. Dulled or burred edges will give you trouble, so keep those edges sharp especially in the spring or under icy conditions.

The base can become damaged by running over small rocks, twigs, etc., especially early in the season when the snow base is not yet deep. These gouges can definitely cause difficulties in maneuverability. A P-tex candle, a metal scraper, a sharply-pointed knife and an electric iron are needed if you'd like to try to do some repairs yourself.

First, with the sharp point of the knife, remove any wax or dirt from the gouges. Then, melt the P-tex candle by holding it against the iron, dripping the wax generously over the gouges. Allow the P-tex to harden, then scrape off the excess with the precision sharpened edge of the steel scraper. You can buy this scraper at a hardware store and sharpen an edge yourself with your file.

The top sides of your skis will be marred if you cross your tips, or stack them in a bus or allow them to fall over. You may want to protect the tops with coats of paste wax. Most manufacturers or ski shops will refinish your ski tops for a price, if and when these evidences of hard usage should really bother you. However, if there is a deep gouge in the top or side surface of a glass ski, it has a tendency to cause accelerated fatigue at that point. Epoxy should be used to seal it.

When storing skis, stand them on the tails in a cool, dry place (except for wood skis which should be clamped together with a block between the bottoms). Use a light coat of oil or grease on metal edges to protect them from rusting. Rust can be removed with fine steel wool.

CARE OF POLES, BINDINGS, AND BOOTS

If you should damage any part of your poles, don't run out to buy new ones. Shafts, baskets, points, handles and straps are easily available at reasonable cost. Once the shaft has been slightly bent by over-stressing, by vigorous usage, or by mishaps, you've weakened it. Slight bends can be removed by pressing the palm against the high point, but don't wedge the pole to force the straightening or use anything with a sharp edge. Nicks or cuts in the shaft will lead to eventual breakage.

Check bindings frequently for loose parts. Once a year, have the bindings checked at a ski shop for proper adjustment and lubrication. Check friction release plates (FRP). These can be bumped loose if only glued on; there is a type that is screwed to the ski. The purpose of the FRP is to allow the boot to release smoothly, so keep this area free of dirt, ice or snow while skiing. A silicone aerosol is a handy lubricant. Check with your ski shop for cold weather lubricants. Store skis with the bindings in their released position.

Molded plastic boots have no exposed stitching which makes them completely trouble free. They do not need to be kept in a boot tree. After skiing, the fasteners should be closed in the position used when skiing, or even tighter. Unless this is done, the boot may be very difficult to adjust the next day. Plastic has a memory; it tends to return to its original flat state Cuts on the inside exteriors of boots occur from contact with ski edges. This occurs even on plastic boots, but does not lessen the functioning of the boot. Buckles are often bent, broken or lost; carry extra buckles with you or have repairs made for a small cost.

An important note to remember while wearing ski boots: they are made for skiing, not walking, and they should be unbuckled even when you are just standing around in them.

Leather boots should be kept in a ski boot tree. After skiing, keep them inside a warm room away from the heater or fireplace. Unlace them until they are dry or mildew will develop inside. Polish frequently with a good wax-base boot polish, never with an oil, which would soften the leather's supportive quality. Seams should be waterproofed with a commercial sealer, ski lacquer or melted cold snow wax. Even a melted candle will suffice as a sealer for a short time.

Chapter 4

SKIING SKILLS

BEGINNING SKILLS

Reading about skiing is not the way to learn the basics, although it has been done. Group or private lessons from a certified ski instructor will be well worth the investment. Friends or relatives seldom have the patience or know the methods to teach efficiently and correctly.

Carrying your skis to the ski school area should not be exhausting if you know how to handle your equipment efficiently. Here are four methods from which to choose:

1 Use fasteners or safety straps to prevent your ski bottoms from slipping apart. Lift skis over your shoulder with tips down. Place poles, held with one hand, over your other shoulder and then under the skis. With a slight downward pressure on the handles, some of the weight is relieved from the other shoulder.

2 Hold skis under one arm, carrying both poles by their handles in the other hand. The poles are now helpful if you are walking on a very slippery surface.

3 If you are walking far, slip the handle of each pole through the basket of the other and the straps over the skis. Now you can carry your skis like a suitcase, leaving one hand free to carry other things.

Four ways to carry skis

4 Interlock the poles by slipping one shaft through the basket of the other, then place the skis between the poles so that the base of the toe piece rests on the poles. With poles over one shoulder, the skis are carried vertically behind your back.

Know Your Equipment

Before reaching the slope, practice getting into and out of your bindings. Know how to fasten the safety straps (safety straps are required at all ski areas to prevent the skis from running away when your bindings release).

To grasp ski poles, slip your hand under the loop, then over the top of the strap, and grip the handle.

Practice lifting one ski, then the other, supporting yourself with your poles. Lift the tips, leaving tails on the snow; lift the tails, leaving tips on the snow. Stand on one ski, pivoting the other around, getting used to the weight on the foot and the amount of action to move the ski.

Walking

Slide skis with bent knees over snow alternately, first without the aid of the poles, letting the arms swing naturally. Then add poles, placing tips of poles at or

Strap over wrist

Grip the handle
Grasping the ski pole

behind the heels of the boots and pushing off with extensions of your arms.

Try for a gliding action from the push off of one ski onto the other. Walk an oval track angling the inside ski slightly, following with the outside ski to change direction. As you become more proficient you may want to try the alternate slide-slide to step-slide, step-slide with a double-pole push off. Change rhythm to a step, step, slide with a double-pole push off.

Tips apart

Tails apart
Stepping around

To step around in a static turn, start with tips on the snow, displace the heels sideways in a pie-shaped angle, close the other ski and continue until facing the opposite direction ("cutting the pie").

Repeat, moving the tips instead of the heels. Be careful not to cross the skis; take small steps ("wagon-wheel").

| Sidestep | Forward sidestep | Herringbone |

Climbing techniques

Climbing

Straight uphill climb   Point ski tips uphill and walk uphill, planting poles behind your heels. Hands are over the tops of the handles, arms straighten with each thrust. This climb is good only on very gentle terrain.

Sidestep   As the terrain steepens, turn your skis across the slope, perpendicular to the fall line (the line a snowball would follow in rolling downhill). Step your ski uphill, placing the uphill edge into the snow by a lateral movement of your knee toward uphill. Stay on the uphill edges. Plant in sequence—uphill pole, uphill ski, downhill ski, downhill pole in rhythm: pole, ski, ski, pole.

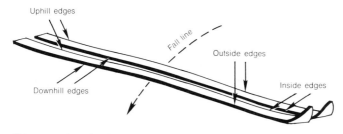

Skis traversing the fall line

Forward sidestep   To the sidestep, add a forward thrust of the uphill ski and close the downhill ski in order to climb diagonally.

Herringbone climb

Herringbone This climbing step is so named because of the pattern it makes in the snow. Facing uphill, place both poles downhill, hands over the tops of the handles, arms straight. Stand with tips apart, tails together on the inside edges, knees leaning inward. Lift one ski over the other, planting it firmly on the inside edge. Continue lifting one ski over the other, supporting with alternate pole thrusts. This climb is usually used for short steep slopes.

Downhill Running

Your body position should be relaxed and natural, as in the athlete's "ready position." Weight is distributed over the balls and heels of the feet, toes flat (there may be a tendency to curl the toes). Ankles are bent and the knees are pressed forward toward the front of the skis. Keep your head up, avoiding the temptation to look down at your ski tips. Focus on something stationary ahead (approximately 20 feet at slow speeds) for better balance and to avoid an accident.

Poles are held at their height, tips projecting backward. Arms are held away from the body at about a 45-degree angle, arms rounded, hands held forward within your peripheral vision. Fore and aft balance is aided by this forward position of the arms. Laterally, the poles are like antennae feeling the snow in light deft movements, giving an added dimension of balance and control. Movement of the poles should be from the wrist in a flicking action.

Hips are forward so that they are in front of, never behind, the heel of your boot. Avoid excessive bending at the waist which will put the weight on the tails of the skis.

Straight running position, profile

Straight running Straight running means moving downhill in the fall line with skis parallel and equally weighted. Push off a level area onto a slight incline with skis in a wide track parallel position (six to eight inches apart). Maintain the same body action as for downhill running. Let the skis run to a stop. Practice knee and ankle flexing, up and down movements while running.

Straight running position, front

Elementary skating step From a straight running position, step the tip of one ski slightly to the side while moving, shift your weight carefully and close the other ski. Repeat until the skis come to a stop.

Falling

When the inevitable happens, relax. Do not try to stop your fall with a hand or by sticking your knee out to the side. Your knee may catch in the snow while the skis continue, resulting in a knee injury. Try to fall to the side and back if you have a choice. Straighten the legs immediately and let your arms straighten out to the sides so the pole will be out of the way.

Falling

Getting Up

Bring your skis parallel and to the downhill side of you. Tuck knees up so your boots are close to your hips. You may have to roll onto your back, lift both skis overhead and then lower them to the downhill side.

Getting up

You may find it easy to stand by simply pushing away from the uphill snow; if not, place your downhill pole in the snow close to your hips on the *uphill* side. With downhill hand holding the pole handle, place your uphill hand on the basket and rock forward until your chest is over the fronts of the skis, then straighten your legs to stand. If you find standing difficult or impossible, you may need to lose some weight, increase leg strength, or both.

Gliding Wedge

This is a fundamental maneuver for controlling speed or stopping at slow speeds. In addition, the maneuver permits the beginner to learn edge control quickly and safely. From a wide track, the tails are displaced

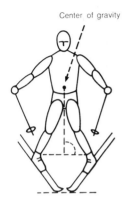

Center of gravity

Gliding wedge

slightly wider than the tips, forming a narrow "V" position.

Preparation On a gentle slope which has an outrun at the bottom, place both poles downhill with hands over the handles and arms straight while turning your skis into the fall line in a slight "V" position.

Body position Keep your knees and ankles moderately flexed, maintaining your body position as in straight running. Weight distribution and edge angle are equal in the fall line.

While running The body is lowered straight down between the skis and edge angle is increased (angle between the ski bottom and the slope) to control your speed. The amount of edging and angling will determine the speed the skis will move.

Stopping Increase the angling of the tails slightly and sink deeper (increased knee bend) between the skis, which increases the edge angle, in order to slow to a stop.

Practice Open to a wedge position from a widetrack parallel, open and close while running; practice a series of small heel thrusts while running in a wedge position. Feel the flattening of the skis when your knees are moved slightly apart. Notice that your knees move inward to re-edge, decreasing speed.

Gliding wedge turn

Gliding Wedge Turn

Your first turns are done in the "V" position in order to learn a braking action and a method of stopping. The skills required—edge control, weight shift, steering and foot turning—will lead to subsequent maneuvers.

Beginning From a straight gliding wedge, press your left knee forward toward the inside. This brings your weight to the ball of the left foot. Maintain a bend in the right knee and release the edge to facilitate sliding. Press forward with the left knee in the desired direction (a right turn).

Completion Steer with the left leg into the desired direction, feeling pressure on the ball of the foot and against the boot in the direction of the turn. Continue edging and steering until the skis turn and slow to a stop across the fall line.

Steering Steering is a turning power caused by a forward, lateral and rotary motion of the knees and a twisting of the feet: Your knees control the movement by shifting laterally toward the desired direction. Avoid any upper body tilting or twisting. Maintain steering throughout the turn. Steering is most effective at the initiation of the turn and most powerful on the outside ski of the turn.

Practice Practice single turns to the right and then to the left. When you can steer in control, combine left and right turns (linked turns).

When you feel fairly confident with the steering action, try steering the inside ski parallel to the outside ski as the turn is finished. If you increase your speed and your skis should skid or slip as the turn is finished, you are beginning to get the feeling of your first christy.

Traverse

To traverse means to descend at an angle to the fall line. Speed increases as the skis are angled more toward downhill. Angle your skis downhill only enough to move slowly.

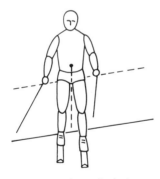

Beginning traverse, center of gravity between skis

Body position Stand with your skis parallel in a wide track (six to eight inches apart). Advance your uphill ski slightly (about two to three inches). Because it is elevated on the slope, your uphill ski will push forward. Poles are held so that a line between them would be parallel to the slope.

Stand with most of your weight on the downhill ski (this should be a natural position). Balance your

Gliding wedge turns

center of gravity so that there is pressure equally distributed on the length of your skis (keep hips forward of heels). Try to obtain a position that would feel comfortable on a 20-mile tour.

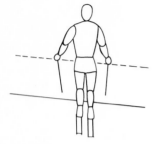

Traverse on a shallow slope

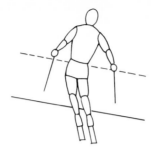

Angulation on a steeper slope

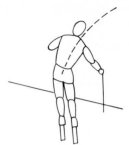

Twisting angulation or anticipation

Traverse position

Running Allow your skis to run on their uphill edges across the slope. Knees are directed laterally toward your uphill side as in the side-step. The amount of angulation of the knees increases as the slope steepness increases. On shallow slopes, there should be only enough upper body angulation to maintain balance.

Stopping Decrease the angle of the traverse in order to come to a stop by either of the following:

Elementary skating uphill While running, lift the uphill tip as in skating and step uphill. Shift weight to the uphill ski and bring the downhill ski alongside. Repeat with very small skating steps away from the fall line until the skis come to a stop. In shifting your weight, take care to maintain your center of gravity over the center of the ski which has the weight.

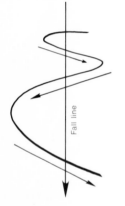

Line of descent, traverse

Skating and steering out of the fall line

Steering uphill Twist the feet and move the knees laterally away from the fall line until the skis begin to turn toward uphill and slow to a stop.

Braking Use an abstem (stemming the downhill ski) or a double stem to a gliding position to slow speed. In an abstem brake, open the downhill ski to brake and return to a traverse. Never brake with the uphill ski alone since this leads to poor body positioning.

Natural or Hockey Stop

From a straight running position, there is a displacement of the skis across the fall line which results in skidding to a stop. It is similar to a sliding stop on ice skates. In skiing this action is referred to as slipping. The slipping action of the hockey stop is used with traversing to learn sideslipping. In more advanced skiing this braking slip is used to control speed in the traverse.

Begin in a wide track straight running position on the fall line in a crouch. The arms are farther forward than usual, poles gripped firmly, baskets extended backward. In a single movement, pivot the skis abruptly across the fall line. Weight the tails of your skis by lowering your center of gravity, as in a sitting position. The upper body remains facing downhill throughout the maneuver.

Become familiar with the slipping action by extending the slip to several yards. Keep the ankles relaxed and stay low in the seated position.

Kickturn

The kickturn is used to turn to face the opposite direction. It requires flexibility, a well-balanced position, control and especially good knee ligaments. It is useful when snow conditions are hazardous or on narrow, steep slopes where a change of direction is desired. A combination of traverse/kickturn/traverse might be used when the steepness of the slope is beyond the skier's ability. (The name KT-22 [22 kickturns] originated for a slope at Squaw Valley, California.)

From a traverse position, twist torso to face downhill, placing both poles uphill behind you, arms straight, hands over the pole handles. From this tripod position, practice kicking the downhill ski so that the heel is placed at the tip of the uphill ski. When the heel is in place, contract the muscles around the knee and

Natural or hockey stop

Kickturn

slowly lower the ski tip until the downhill ski is parallel and facing the opposite direction to the uphill ski.

Turn your upper body toward the new direction, placing the uphill pole downhill and forward. Bring the uphill ski around, taking care not to hit the downhill pole.

With practice, this maneuver can be completed in two moves without placing the tail of the downhill ski in the snow. There are other variations of the kickturn but this one is the most practical.

Sideslip

In the sideslip the skis are allowed to slip sideways down the slope by flattening the edges of the skis.

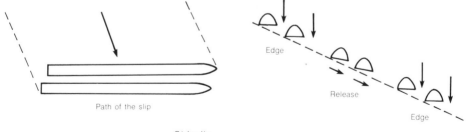

Path of the slip

Edge

Release

Edge

Sideslip

From a standing position The cautious skier can learn to release the edges from a standing position on a fairly steep but short slope. Plant both poles away from the skis at each side for balance. Climb up to the uphill pole and slip down to the downhill pole.

Release the edges by moving your knees away from their uphill position until they are just over the boot. Keep more weight on the downhill ski and bend the knees and ankles (do not rise up to release the edges). Face the direction of the movement (downhill) with the upper body. Angle your upper body laterally to maintain balance. This turning of the upper body, combined with twisting angulation is called "anticipation."

From a wedge position From a wedge position, moving across a shallow slope, bring the uphill ski parallel to the lower ski. The skis will slip if your ankles and feet are relaxed and if you sink deeper as the skis are brought parallel.

From a traverse position While moving in a shallow traverse (skis parallel, wide track), the edges will release slightly as the knees are relaxed away from their "into the hill" position. The skis will slip forward and sideways. Steer the feet so that the skis turn into the hill to a shallower traverse or to a stop. Edges are reset with a lateral knee movement into the hill. The amount of slippage is controlled by the amount of edging.

Beginning Basic Christy

The basic beginning christy is a combination of a traverse, a gliding wedge turn and a forward sideslip or skid. The skier has already learned to slip, to move the length of the ski laterally. Next, the beginning skier must experience a skid in which the tail moves laterally more than the tip. The purpose is to carve the turn, to round out any size radius of turn with a minimum of slippage or skidding. Skidding is caused by resistance against the tip as edging is increased (along with centrifugal force, forward leaning or leverage, and side camber). Carving occurs with these forces plus a refinement of proper weighting, edging, body positioning and leg action (steering with the feet and knees).

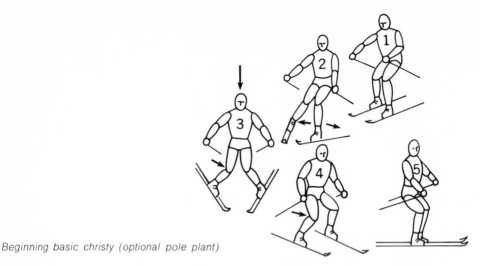

Beginning basic christy (optional pole plant)

Preparation Increased speed is necessary to encourage the skidding phase at the end of each turn, so practice the gliding wedge at higher speeds.

Traverse, turn, skid Traverse, open the skis to a wedge by pushing out the lower ski or both skis. Shift your weight to the uphill ski. Increase the edging and steer into the fall line. Continue past the fall line, bringing the inside ski parallel to the outside ski. Maintain a wide track and stay low in the knees between the skis. Steer the skis further out of the fall line into a skid, rounding out the slippage. Practice turns in both directions.

Beginning basic christy

Use of the pole Bring the inside pole (downhill pole) forward preparing to place it in the snow. As you prepare to bring the inside ski parallel, plant your pole forward and to the side (about halfway between the ski tip and the bindings) turning around your pole. Pretend that your elbow is in a cast so that the pole must be planted with a bending of the knees. The pole plant and the bringing of the skis to parallel will occur earlier as you become more proficient and ski at increased speeds. The pole plant becomes increasingly essential for rhythm, balance and unweighting.

Practice When practicing at a slower speed, use a wide stem and begin to steer the outside ski immediately. When increasing the speed of the maneuver, stem the skis narrower and bring them parallel earlier, stepping to the outside ski in order to unweight and change the edge of the inside ski.

Turn over bumps to facilitate turns. Bumps will aid in unweighting or lightening the skis which will ease the turning. After you have been skiing over bumps and changes of terrain at higher speeds you will be able to increase your foot sensitivity. Absorb changes in the terrain beneath you by relaxing knees, ankles and body.

Always focus your eyes ahead of you, farther down the slope as your speed increases. Keep your hands well forward within your field of vision. Keep your arms rounded and away from the body. Never allow your arms to hang back in the turn.

*Uphill christy
viewed from the uphill side*

Uphill Christy

An uphill christy is merely a forward sideslip with a curve in it, a curve which rounds into the hill. You might have achieved this curving action fairly well when learning the forward sideslip and the basic christy. In any event, let's review it again since all christies end in a rounded sideslip to some degree.

Practice a rounded sideslip from a shallow traverse. Exaggerate the down motion and the steering as both knees deepen forward and into the hill.

Body position Press your knees forward by bending at the ankles, giving more weight to the front of the skis if they should fail to turn. If you are overturning into the hill, decrease the forward leaning, assuming a more relaxed position in the knees.

Timing and steering The radius of the turn depends on the timing of the down motion and the steering, applied gradually for longer radius turns, applied quickly for short radius turns. If your uphill ski doesn't want to come around, try turning on the downhill ski only, steering with the downhill leg, feeling pressure on the inside of the downhill foot. Practice from a gliding wedge across the hill, changing the inside edge of the uphill ski by steering this ski parallel to the downhill ski.

Practice Practice uphill christies with a pole plant to aid in balance and timing.

Uphill christies can finish with forward skidding, a continuing traverse or a stop. Practice all of these.

Intermediate Basic Christy

Ski schools that use the abstem (stemming the lower ski) suggest that this method tends to diminish the probability of developing an uphill stemming habit and that the downhill stem leads naturally to the check and to a platform for rebounding. For these reasons the abstem method is included. Many instructors will disagree, contending that a double stem is smoother and easier to perform requiring less body and muscular motion. Since the student is already familiar with the double stem it seems more natural. Students who are less cautious may benefit by omitting the abstem christy, moving directly to skiing faster in wide track parallel. However, the check must still be learned, first with the downhill ski and then with both skis to learn "setting." Rebound turns or "jet" turns are the student's ultimate goal.

Still in a widetrack stance, ski with increased speed linking turns rhythmically. The abstem aids in

Intermediate basic christy

changing the edge of the uphill ski and creates a platform from which to push off or a point from which to rebound. In the intermediate level of the christy, the skis are brought parallel when the skis are in the fall line. The closing or bringing to a parallel position occurs earlier (before entering the fall line) in the more advanced basic christy with a stem.

Preparation   While standing in a traverse position, push the lower ski out, step back to the uphill ski, pushing off the abstemmed ski. Do the same while moving. Try a complete turn using a bump in the terrain. The bump adds lift, unweighting the skis for ease of turning.

Use of the pole   In the sinking or abstem phase, the pole comes forward and as the edge is set, the pole is planted. As you come up and bring your skis parallel, the pole aids in up-unweighting, stabilizes and propels you into the turn.

Decrease the stem   Attempt to decrease the amount of stem, but increase the amount of push-off and steering after bringing the skis parallel.

Steering   When stepping onto the outside ski, pivot it with a strong steering action and forward pressure to control the skid.

Uphill stem   If the snow is sticky or mushy, use slow speeds and use an uphill stem instead of an abstem.

Intermediate Basic Christy Exercises

Gliding wedge *wedeln (veduln)* or *wedel (vedul)*
In the fall line, steer the skis in very short linked rhythmical gliding wedge turns. Then try picking up the inside ski. When you can achieve this, attempt to bring the inside ski parallel to the outside ski.

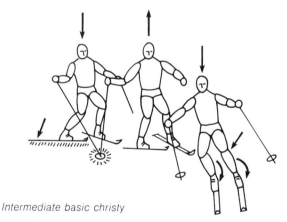

Intermediate basic christy

Abstem garlands From a traverse, abstem and turn into the fall line. Use an uphill pole plant, unweight, shift weight back to the abstemmed ski and finish with a christy uphill (no crossing of the fall line). The pivotal point should be near the toe of the foot. Maintain a wide track. Repeat, linking turns together. A series of turns resemble a garland design in the snow. In later practices, let the uphill ski join the skid during the abstem checking.

Pre-turn or check   Practice longer radius turns across the hill with a pole plant. With practice you will soon be able to let the uphill ski skid into a closer parallel position a (pre-turn or check). Emphasize weighting the outside ski.

Moguls or bumps   Attempt to turn directly over the top of the moguls to aid in the unweighting and foot steering. Keep your weight on the outside ski. Get the idea of this action by standing on a bump with tips and tails off the snow. Plant the inside (downhill) pole for balance and steer the feet in the direction of the desired turn. Absorb bumps by flexing knees and checking speed on the top of the bumps, extending legs as the skis slide down the sides. Maintain the torso facing downhill. Do not allow the body to rotate in the direction of the tips, although some anticipation with the hips is helpful if done properly. Avoid wide stemming; slow down by sideslipping on the downhill sides of the moguls.

Advanced Basic Christy

At this point you are probably skiing parallel most of the time. The following discussion will help you to eliminate or at least to diminish any stem you may have.

Advanced basic christy

Advanced basic christy

Anticipation Using moguls and wide track, your stem becomes less obvious. Emphasize anticipation before the turn. While you are finishing one turn you are anticipating the next. With slow speeds and short radius turns you will need a strong emphasized anticipation. As speed increases and turns become longer in radius your anticipation is lessened and becomes more subtle.

Eliminating the stem Some stemming will probably become evident in the downhill ski as a result of the action of anticipation. With more emphasis on pushing off the pole and emphasis on body tilting in the direction of the turn this stemming will be eliminated. Sink with slightly more weight on the downhill ski in the pre-turn (skidding both skis to an edge set). Come off the edge set of both skis simultaneously (treating both skis as one) onto both skis, weighting both skis equally at the beginning, increasing weight on the outside ski throughout the turn.

Steering The slower the turn, the more the knees must work to pull the skis into the turn.

Parallel christy

Parallel Christy

From a traverse, edges are set with a down motion and a pole-plant. With an up-motion the edges are changed simultaneously as the skis are steered toward the fall line. Centrifugal force immediately pulls the skis to the outside. This pull is resisted by the skis because of the friction against the snow caused by edging. This resistance is caused by side camber and forward leverage which is greatest at the tip and results in a turn. The pull of gravity which increases as the skis pass the fall line is controlled by edging. Steering completes the turn and skier is sinking in preparation for the next turn.

Review of Unweighting

The reduction or elimination of the skier's weight against the snow can be accomplished in the following ways:

Up-unweighting   The action of rising from a lowered position or the moving from an angular position to an extended one.

Down-unweighting   Dropping the body quickly while bending at the knees, ankles and hips, or dropping into an angular position (as in the sideslip and later, in advanced skiing, *avalement*). Note that reduction of weight lasts longer at the top of the "up" than the bottom of the "down."

Pole-plant   The pushing off of the pole plant aids in

reducing the skier's weight. Keep arms forward within the field of vision and avoid unnecessary arm movements.

Moguls or bumps   Turning on the top of a bump adds lift. Retract the legs on bump to unweight skis.

Edge set check (pre-turn)   The abstem and later the simultaneous edge set of both skis creates a platform from which to rebound. The relaxation of the legs and deangulation of the body immediately after the edge set affords a sudden lightening of the skis, a recoiling action.

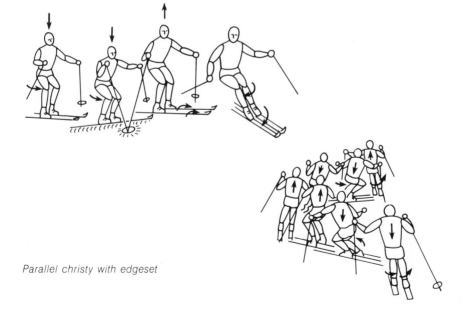

Parallel christy with edgeset

Corrections of Common Errors

Stiff downhill leg Avoid trying to brake throughout your turns, except in the gliding wedge. Check before the turn, then let the skis glide without forcing through the turn. Treat the snow gently. Also, a stiff downhill leg may be caused by excessive weighting of the outside ski.

Overturning or turning too abruptly Have confidence that the skis will turn. Don't try to turn immediately out of the fall line or you will throw yourself off balance and overturn, making the next turn difficult. Tails will overturn and the downhill arm may cross the front of the body at the end of the turn. To correct this, stay in the fall line, keeping skis flat a little longer than you think you should. Check your speed *before* the turn and round out the slippage smoothly through each turn. Avoid excessive arm and body movements. Let your skis and legs do the turning, not the hips or arms or upper body.

Leaning into the hill Leaning uphill usually accompanies a straight downhill leg. Each will cause the other. Lack of confidence will cause some skiers to seek a more comfortable feeling by leaning toward the slope during a traverse, especially on steep slopes. This puts weight on the uphill ski resulting in an unstable position. The firm edging achieved by increased angulation (weight over the downhill ski, dropping the downhill shoulder, knees and hips into the slope) will give the timid skier confidence to ski steeper on icy slopes. Keep your edges sharpened. Have your equipment checked to see if the base and edges are satisfactory. If you have difficulty holding an edge in a traverse, you may need canting (installation of tilting material) within or on your boots or skis.

Lack of aggressiveness The skier who makes timid, weak movements, where firm, precise and dynamic movements are required will never reach an advanced level of skill. Skiing demands aggressiveness, quickness and precision. Through experience you must learn a kinesthetic awareness of body position. The timid skier tends to sit back or lean too far forward. Try to find your proper balance position, neither always on the balls of the feet nor on the heels. As your skill increases you will find the need for constant shifts of weight forward and backward during maneuvers. Develop foot sensitivity.

Skiers who lack aggressiveness usually just touch at the snow with their poles, in what should be firm, precise pole-plants. The pole aids in unweighting if done properly, as well as in spotting the turn.

Skiing at slow speeds actually impedes the learning process. Practice checking from a fast forward side-slip on a steep slope. Attempt to ski faster with precise movements. Avoid turning too far across the fall line. Avoid too much traversing between turns. The end of one turn is the beginning of the next. Try to develop rhythm in linking your turns.

ADVANCED SKILLS

Straight Running

Considerable practice in straight running or schussing on uneven terrain at greater speeds is necessary at this point in your progress. As you develop foot sensitivity to terrain changes you are also increasing your skill in body positioning and edge control.

Keep your weight distributed over the whole of your foot, body flexed ready to absorb and to extend. Hands are held low, skis apart and parallel. A very slight inside edging will aid in tracking at higher speeds. Schuss with increasing speeds as you gain confidence. The amount of flex in the body can vary from high open standing to the lowest—the "egg position is called the "bullet," which is a less stable position in rough terrain because there is decreased ability in absorbing shocks.

Egg position

Absorbing bumps is often called *avalement,* a French word meaning swallowing, literally swallowing the bumps by retraction of the legs and contraction of the stomach muscles. If the bump is too high to swallow this way, the feet can be pushed forward at the moment the mogul is met, which increases the absorption. After the mogul, pull your feet back under you quickly.

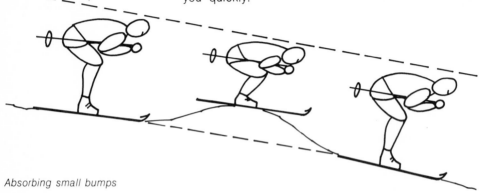

Absorbing small bumps

In meeting bumps at high speeds you may easily be airborne. Staying on the snow is safer and, in racing, faster. To avoid loss of contact with the snow, extend the body rapidly just before the bump, retracting the legs on the bump so that the bump will not afford a lift.

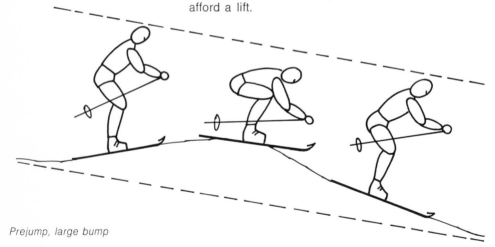

Prejump, large bump

A christy stop is a quick stopping maneuver used on a narrow trail or catwalk or when an obstacle or another skier offers no other choice. From a widetrack schuss, both skis are pivoted forceably to a position across the fall line, as in the hockey stop. The entire body flexes suddenly and forcibly, body facing downhill. Pressure is exerted on the tails as the skis are skidding. As you sink deeper into a crouch with your body angulated over the outside ski, force your knees into the hill for a rapid edge set. This edge set will flip you over downhill or let you fall sideways into the hill unless your body angulates. Your downhill pole can be planted at the exact moment of edge set with upper body angulation for added balance.

Beginning Jet Turns

The beginning jet turn is not an accelerating turn. It is merely an edge set which stops lateral movement, but allows forward movement. Edge setting creates a rebound effect (unweighting) which is absorbed by the legs through relaxation. This results in the skis jetting forward. The upper body, anticipating the direction the skis will eventually travel, allows the skis to be brought into alignment. The turn is completed with pressure on the front of the skis, foot steering and proper edging. Reaching more downhill with your pole plant is necessary.

Before practicing this turn, you should have reviewed and now feel fairly confident with your timing and pole plant in the parallel christy and the preturn with both skis.

Rounded turns Your instructor will want you to round out your turns more with a smoother and more gradual sinking and edge set.

Anticipation The change of angulation to the other side must be started right after the rebound. Your instructor will stress the importance of angulation and anticipation.

Carving your turns As your skis begin to carve better (increased pressure on tips with a good balance between the amount of edging and steering), you will find your skis coming closer together.

Recovery phase Remember, jetting is not sitting back, contrary to popular belief. The photos and posters you see of skiers in the recovery phase definitely do give this illusion.

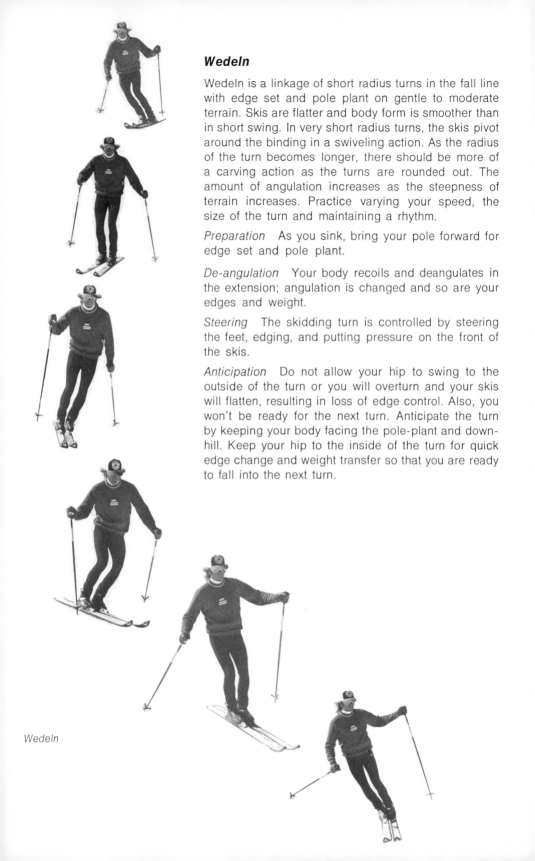

Wedeln

Wedeln is a linkage of short radius turns in the fall line with edge set and pole plant on gentle to moderate terrain. Skis are flatter and body form is smoother than in short swing. In very short radius turns, the skis pivot around the binding in a swiveling action. As the radius of the turn becomes longer, there should be more of a carving action as the turns are rounded out. The amount of angulation increases as the steepness of terrain increases. Practice varying your speed, the size of the turn and maintaining a rhythm.

Preparation   As you sink, bring your pole forward for edge set and pole plant.

De-angulation   Your body recoils and deangulates in the extension; angulation is changed and so are your edges and weight.

Steering   The skidding turn is controlled by steering the feet, edging, and putting pressure on the front of the skis.

Anticipation   Do not allow your hip to swing to the outside of the turn or you will overturn and your skis will flatten, resulting in loss of edge control. Also, you won't be ready for the next turn. Anticipate the turn by keeping your body facing the pole-plant and downhill. Keep your hip to the inside of the turn for quick edge change and weight transfer so that you are ready to fall into the next turn.

Wedeln

Wedeln

Shortswing

Shortswing refers to linked christies executed with *avalement* or jetting on moderate to steep slopes. There is a more definite check, pole plant and anticipation. All of your previous skills must be practiced and perfected, such as: (a) Forward sideslipping with changes from edge set to release to edge set. (b) Keeping your hips into the hill as you are accentuating the down motion to set your edges for anticipation of the turn. (c) Untwisting from the edge set, relaxing the edges, and "blocking" (stopping your untwisting motion by strong abdominal muscular contraction), which pulls the skis into alignment with your upper body. (d) Pivoting your skis around the binding (not around the tips), staying on the edges, minimizing the slippage. (e) In steep terrain, practicing double pole-plants for increasing balance.

Shortswing

1-2 Turning out of fall line, sink into edgeset and pole plant, keeping upper body facing downhill;

2-3 With edges set and pole planted, body recoils from the compression, ski edges begin to flatten;

3-4 Body deangulates and blocks; legs are relaxed to bring skis into alignment with upper body;

5-6 Body begins sinking, steering and changing to the new angulation as pole swings forward for next pole-plant.

Problems in shortswing Too much uphill ski lead could be caused by "tibial torsion" (a bowing of the lower leg). This results in the downhill knee tucking behind the uphill knee. Correct by canting boots or skis. (Adjustments of the bindings must be made.) Have your alignment checked by a ski shop that offers this service. Some boots have a cant adjustment.

Too much forward lean results in overturning around the tip of the skis instead of around the binding. Re-practice stop christies, sinking deeper into the edge set on your entire foot, not on the ball of the foot.

Do not allow your poles to fall back out of your line of sight or they will be late for the next turn. Plant your pole further forward at higher speeds.

Do not allow the hips to turn in the direction of the skis. Keep your hips aligned in the direction of the upper body.

Your upper body should not appear to be moving up or down, twisting, etc. Keep your upper body quiet and make the legs do the turning. The upper body movement is merely balancing and compensating for changes by the lower body.

Avalement

As you know, *avalement* is not a turn but it is a way of initiating a turn. The act of swallowing bumps by retracting the legs unweights the skis, allowing a change of direction. Exaggeration of *avalement* results in sitting back. Remember to tip the upper body forward quickly in the direction you wish to turn to maintain balance.

To initiate the *avalement,* head for the bump on a 45-degree angle. Your upper body faces the pole plant. The upper body is stabilized by an abdominal contraction. This stopping of torsional body movement is called "blocking". Steer the turn, legs retracting to absorb the bump (jetting skis slightly will help absorb larger moguls). Extend legs and align skis with upper body. The radius of the turn depends on the amount of edging and the amount of pressure on the front of the skis.

Avalement can be used without bumps by turning the skis a bit more uphill. Your body must be strongly anticipated, legs greatly compressed as the edges are released and the skis are pulled into the turn. If enough absorption is not allowed in the legs, this edge set, far across the fall line, will rebound you off balance.

On very large moguls, approach the bump at the last moment with your body extended, now you can absorb the bump with your greatest amount of contraction. *Avalement* is used in deep snow as well. Emphasis is on retracting and jetting the feet forward to allow the skis to skim to the surface.

Challenging Conditions

Deep powder snow   This type of snow is not recommended for the novice. Until you have the daring and the skill, stay on the packed slopes. Do not ski powder alone. It is possible to fall in really deep snow and not be able to get up. If this should happen, lay your ski poles on the snow in a criss-cross design, place your hand over the cross and push off. On open slopes, look for avalanche hazard signs, and in wooded areas, remove pole straps from your wrists.

With proper equipment you will have more fun. Use goggles that do not fog and allow snow to blow into the ventilation cracks. Select clothes that are easily brushed clear of snow with no "gaposis" at the waist. Over-the-boot pants or gaiters (elasticized overcuffs) help keep snow from entering the front of your boots. Softer skis of a lesser sidecut are best but your regular skis will probably be versatile enough unless they are very stiff in the tip. On special powder skis, bindings are set slightly back of normal placement.

Try a few uphill christies before heading downhill in order to get the feel of the snow. Some deep snow will allow little or no rebound. Some will have a breakable crust on top and will be fluffy below. Take care.

You will have the greatest advantage using skis designed for powder. With most regular skis, you will have to keep slightly more weight on the tails. Continuous weight back and too much weight back prevents swiveling. This is a poor method of skiing powder. Weight should balance over the length of the ski, never extremely forward or backward. Keep weight equal on both skis and lower your weight by assuming a sitting position (do not bend over at the waist). The outside ski may be weighted lightly for security in changing conditions

Try to ski close to the fall line on a shallow slope. Turn only enough to control your speed.

Short radius turns *Avalement* and anticipation are used in short radius turns. The upper body remains quiet but the arms may be raised upward and forward during up-unweighting. Plant your pole earlier and use hip projection (starting the hip into the desired direction), transferring the turning power to the legs.

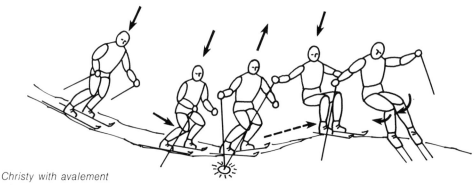

Christy with avalement

Forward and up (anticipation and directional projection)

Long radius turns A greatly exaggerated down-up motion is used in single turns or long radius turns. As you develop a greater sense of balance and are able to stay closer to the fall line, you will be able to refine your movements eliminating hip rotation and large arm projections. Try an *avalement* at the end of the up-motion with a projection of the skis to the outside of the turn. The up-motion will diminish and eventually disappear as *avalement* is increased. *Avalement* may be used in any size turn.

Learn first on shallow terrain, staying in the fall line, turning only enough to change direction, and not so much that you lose momentum. Steeper slopes will definitely "psych" you out if you do not learn first on shallow slopes.

Ice Every skier will occasionally find himself having to ski icy slopes. You may have some misconceptions about how to handle slick slopes, and after trying it you may wonder if it is even possible. Accept the opportunity to learn how to ski ice or frozen corn snow. These suggestions will help you face the hazards of skiing ice.

Always file your skis before skiing ice.

Do not over-turn or your skis will slip sideways.

Do not exaggerate forward leaning. Stay in the center of your feet (even pressure throughout the length of the ski).

Edge with knee action and *do not overedge* or make abrupt edge sets, especially across the fall line.

Keep skis on the snow, unweighting very little since your skis will tend to overturn.

Never "bank" your turns (leaning to the inside of the turn with no angulation).

Put pressure on tails at the end of your turns.

When edges are lost and slipping occurs, use internal turning forces to initiate a quick turn. (A displacement of one part of the body brings about an equal but opposite displacement of another part.)

Use the uphill side of moguls as platforms to turn on.

Widen your base by holding skis in a moderately wide track.

Moguls Bumps should be skied with *"joie de vivre,"* with a fun-seeking attitude. It takes quite a lot of frustrating effort before you reach this point of exhilarating adventure, but it is there for you to discover. Go looking for bumps before your legs become tired and learn to master short stretches of small bumpy terrain before you try the big steep!

Keep your body facing downhill. Stay low with your arms well forward, ready for quick moves.

Look ahead and plan your line. Concentrate on the turns well ahead, never on the turn you are making. Following close behind an instructor will give you courage and will teach you how to choose the proper line.

Absorb bumps with your knees. Do not allow the bumps to lift you airborne by accident. Occasionally, jump playfully on purpose from the top of one mogul to the downhill side of the next.

Turn your skis enough to control speed but do not go into a traverse.

Turn on the uphill side of the bump and ski through the valley.

Be aggressive.

Let the terrain determine your rhythm. Moguls made by experts are much easier and more fun than those made by beginners, who are cutting across the hill causing bumps with sharp downhill sides and no rhythmic spacing.

Changes in snow Running from mushy soft snow in the sun into icy harder snow in the shade will occur often in spring skiing. Adaptable positioning is necessary. When approaching an icy spot, anticipate increased speed under you, thrusting one ski slightly forward to increase the length of your base and lean forward. Conversely, approaching slush, thrust one ski backward and lean back slightly to avoid being thrown forward off balance.

Corn snow Snow crystals in spring weather have lost the star-like points of their original structure through melting and refreezing. The result resembles smooth kernels which flow under the skis as if they were ball-bearings. Unless the weather becomes too warm or the snow is exposed too directly to the sun, these corn kernels persist and can be very enjoyable and easy to ski.

Ski lightly, riding the skis gently.

Avoid heavy edge sets and strong up-and-down movements.

Make turns closer to the fall line. Check your tracks. Wide traverses indicate you are skiing with too much motion. See diagram.

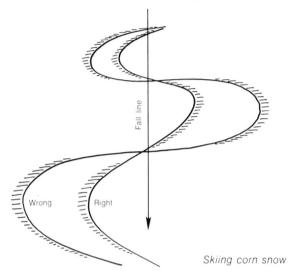

Skiing corn snow

"Skiing the crud" This term refers to breakable crust or mushy heavy snow or a combination of seemingly impossible conditions most often found in the spring. Those who go looking for "junk" to ski have truly learned to master their skis and dote on letting everyone know it.

Some suggestions for those aggressors of the rough:

Use a tail hop to initiate turns (sometimes called a *"ruade"*). This is energetic but it is a safe motion. Use double pole plants. Do not attempt to hop your whole body. The upper body remains quiet, legs retract, lifting the heels only. Land with tips in the fall line, skis equally weighted. Exert the greatest turning force as the skis break through. Continue steering with just enough weight on the uphill ski so that it will not be deflected by the snow's resistance.

Use split-rotation which affords additional turning

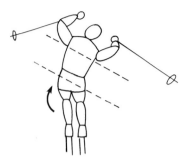

Parallel axis of hips and shoulders

power to overcome the greater resistance of this kind of snow. Start with an up and forward projection of the outside arm and hip. Block the upper body movement by contracting strongly with abdominal muscles, transferring turning power to the legs to pull the skis into the fall line. Finish the turn with a counter-motion, reversing the upper body from the direction of the turn.

In very hazardous conditions, use an exaggerated form of compression-extension turn. Effective hip movement requires that the axis of the shoulders and hips be kept parallel. The hips move inward to the center of the turn after blocking to create an effective edge set.

SUMMARY

You have already discovered that there are many kinds of turns, depending on the terrain, the student's ability and the kind of snow. Some of these turns were transitional and essential to learning how to ski. Here is a review of the methods already discussed:

Steered turn The skier puts his weight on the outside ski, using it to steer into his new direction. This enables the beginner to control his speed and can be done without up unweighting and the coordination of upper and lower body which is required in the more advanced turns.

Step turn or elementary skating step The skier, slowly downhill, steps one tip away from the fall line, closes the downhill ski and effects a change of direction.

Racer's step turn The racer uses a similar movement in a different way for maintaining a higher approach to a gate. He steps uphill pushing off the downhill ski for acceleration onto the uphill ski, putting it on its new edge as he closes the downhill ski, steering into the turn.

Foot swivel off a bump Skier approaches the bump with the upper body facing downhill, body contracts at top of the bump, tails and tips are off the snow; feet are twisted into the new direction.

Jet turn The skier anticipates the turn with his upper body, edge sets and pushes his skis forward. Pressure of the skis on the snow is thereby released and the feet are swiveled into the turn.

Aerial turns   A way to overcome the resistance of the skis on the snow is to let a bump lift you and swivel the skis into the fall line while airborne. Land with tips lower than tails. Let leg flexion soften the landing and apply just enough edge to hold the finish of the turn. Legs may be tucked or extended while airborne.

Turn with *avalement*   As the skier approaches a bump, he retracts his legs, accentuating the jetting action, and steers into the turn.

Ruade   Using both poles, the skier leans forward, kicks up both tails displacing them to the side. This is used for difficult snow conditions or a narrow chute.

NEW-OLD TURNS

Here are some other turns which still linger from techniques of bygone eras. All are still useful in various situations and you will still see them on the slopes.

Pure rotation   A down-motion initiates the turn; the torso rotates into the intended direction. To transmit this turning power from the upper body to the skis, the abdominal muscles are contracted (the hips are "blocked"). The arm and shoulder lead the rotation, but the blockage of the movement is important so that over-rotation does not occur. This turn may be used in all kinds of deep snow, from powder to crud.

Pure reverse or counter-rotation   This turn is explained by Isaac Newton's third law: for every action there is an opposite and equal reaction. As the skier rises to unweight he rotates his legs downhill and opposes this action by turning upper body uphill or away from the intended direction. This results in an exaggerated angulation or comma position which affords excellent edging and carving ability. It is not satisfactory in snow of any great resistance. It is best for quick changes of direction in tight bumps and in quick turns in slalom.

Split rotation   This turn was mentioned earlier in the discussion of skiing the crud. The split can be made two ways: begin with rotation and as the turn progresses the skier reverses his shoulders from the intended direction. Or the turn may be initiated with a reverse shoulder or counter-rotation, then completed with a rotation of the upper body to finish square with the skis.

Mambo This is a rhythmical series of turns on a shallow smooth slope in which the skier over-rotates until the skis are going one way and the shoulders are going the other. An extreme reverse shoulder position is followed immediately by the next turn, arms held shoulder high and wide. Skis seem to snake and the body defies gravity; done just for fun.

Banked turn This is a turn in which the skier edges the skis in the desired direction and leans into the turn. The design of the ski allows the ski to turn simply by edging and giving weight to the skis as they meet the snow's resistance. This turn is used for high speed long turns on packed slopes, in powder, or in terrain where gullies afford side slopes to ride up and bank from.

***Reuel* christy** This is a turn on the inside ski with the downhill ski lifted sideways high off the snow. The upper body leans forward and arms are extended as needed for balance; a beautiful and graceful turn done to express sheer exhilaration.

CORRECTIONS OF COMMON ERRORS

Stemming Developing a pure parallel turn, whether wide-track or not, is important to the skier. Even a slight stem is regarded as undesirable. Skiing with a stem in heavy or unpacked snow, powder snow or moguls is hazardous.

When the uphill ski stems first and the other ski closes you have a problem. Try to kick the habit by skiing wide-track, setting edges to check speed, coming off both skis simultaneously onto both skis, weighting them equally. If you learned to check with a downhill stem, this should be fairly easy. If you have learned to check with an uphill stem, try an abstem check at lower speeds. Come up and forward as you unweight and steer your feet into the turn.

Throwing the hip Too often a good skier has trouble learning *wedeln* because he tries to force the outside hip into the direction of the turn. In *wedeln* the hip stays to the inside of the turn, the upper body remains facing downhill. The legs turn the skis and the hips move inside away from the feet. Feet and leg muscles steer the skis.

There are maneuvers in which the hip moves up and forward in the unweighting (to initiate a turn in heavy or deep snow); however, there is a stopping of the movement. If the hip is not stopped, the skier will be off-balance, leaning into the hill on the uphill ski.

In anticipation, there is a slight movement of the hip toward the direction of the turn but it is only at the beginning as the body recoils from the edge set. The hip must move immediately to the inside to angulate again.

Controlling speed It is necessary to maintain proper body position in order to check effectively with edge sets. Some bad habits are: too much weight on the uphill ski, arms too close to the body, arms hanging back late in the turn. You must be ready to set quickly and aggressively at any time, especially at increased speeds and in bumps. In *wedeln* or short swing, your arms must be well forward to plant one pole as soon as the other leaves the snow. Do not allow your arm to be pulled past your shoulder; work poles from your wrists.

Set your edges on the top flat part of moguls, using pole-plants for balance (not for unweighting or you will be thrown airborne). When skiing through moguls in the valleys you must carve the skis or you will accelerate. The outside ski takes most of the weight in the edge set (about two-thirds). Skis that are too stiff in the tips for your weight will probably be difficult to ski in moguls. They can cause the skier to accelerate into an out-of-control traverse.

If you find yourself traversing, unable to pick a line or a spot to begin a turn, it may be your body position. Are you really ready—downhill pole forward in position for planting and upper body anticipating, already facing toward the valley? Picking a line is easier if you learn by following an instructor or someone who is an expert in the moguls. Your leader must ski at a speed within your ability so that you can keep up and copy his rhythm and timing. Learn quick edge sets and reaction-set turns.

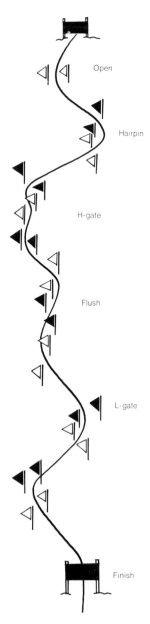

Open

Hairpin

H-gate

Flush

L-gate

Finish

Gates used in slalom

COMPETITION

Whether or not you seriously consider yourself the racing type, you'll enjoy watching competitors if you know what is involved. Do not discount the benefits of racing techniques. They will improve your free skiing tremendously.

The Alpine events are classified as slalom, giant slalom and downhill. Nordic events are jumping and cross-country. Ski clubs and ski schools usually sponsor competitions for the enjoyment and education of their members. Universities, colleges and high schools afford opportunities for inter-scholastic competition where skiing conditions are within reach. Your regional ski association, which sanctions races, will give you information on how to get a race card so that you can earn points as a classified competitor. With a Class C card you will try to earn enough points to advance to B, then A. Youngsters are classified according to age and ability.

Slalom This is very popular with spectators because there is a lot of action and most of the course can be seen easily. Learning to ski slalom will stimulate aggressiveness, agility and reaction reflexes. Shorter, softer skis with increased sidecut are used, making the ski hug the contours and react quickly. A course is composed of matched flags of alternate colors which comprise gates, set two to three feet apart. The racer must pass through the gates with both feet. If he should miss a gate or split a pole, he must hike back up until both feet are between the poles, then he may continue.

Poles may be knocked down without penalty. These rules are true in Giant Slalom and Downhill, but in those events, speeds are usually too great to allow for backing up if a gate is missed. The racer would be scored DNF (did not finish). In the Slalom and Giant Slalom, the skier is never allowed to ski through the course or even to shadow it. He must hike up the course to memorize the gates, then sideslip the course and hike up again until he is sure of each combination in succession. Some combinations are: open, closed, hairpin, H-gate or Seelos, flush and L-gate.

The only way to learn racing is to practice under the auspices of an experienced coach, one who has competed himself and knows how to teach. Technique along with quickness and agility are emphasized in Slalom.

Giant slalom Originally the giant slalom was designed as a baby downhill. However, the skills involved require the best of the downhill and the best of the slalom. There are from 50 to 70 gates, about 20 feet apart. The racer must study the course and choose the fastest line that he can hold. There must be a minimum of slipping since the edged ski moves faster in its track than when slipping. In both slalom and giant slalom, the racer uses an uphill step and turn for increased speed. By stepping uphill before the gate he can increase the steepness of his line and cut closer to the gate. Sometimes the turn is finished on the uphill ski so that the line may be held. Any skier will enjoy learning and using this turn.

There are seldom opportunities to practice giant slalom and downhill since they require such great speeds and most recreational areas do not have closed areas for racing. The best way to learn is to join an area-sponsored-racing club.

Downhill This is the fastest and most physically demanding of the three types. The course follows the terrain: gates are used to control speed just enough to keep the course as safe as possible. Still, it is the most dangerous. The terrain must have a great variety of changes, jumps, bumps, schusses, gullies and steepness. International events are two to three miles in length for men and one to one and one-half miles for women. Length of courses is usually referred to by time, not distance, e.g.: a two-minute course.

Some of the skills you can learn from the downhill racer are the egg tuck position and the pre-jump. The racer must hold the tuck in rough terrain in order to decrease wind resistance and the pre-jump is important to keep the skis on the snow, since being airborne would slow his speed. The rules of course-setting and competing vary according to sex, age, skill and level of racing.

Fun racing with a handicap has been organized nationally in the United States and is called NASTAR (National Standard Race). Some ski area near you will be offering these races on the weekends. Anyone can enter as many times as desired. The purpose— to race against yourself, to improve and to have fun.

A course setter sets the optimal time for that course and you are given a handicap according to your ability. Even beginners may enter. Winners at the end of the season are awarded medals and recognition.

Nordic events Cross-country is enjoying popularity in the U.S., especially since "touring" on skis has recently been given so much emphasis by equipment manufacturers. Advertisements show families getting back to nature while enjoying the winter scenery on skis. Cross-country competition is an Olympic event but is not much of a spectator sport since the course may extend over as much as 10 miles or take an hour or more. As in downhill and giant slalom, racers are started at intervals. They must pass certain check points between start and finish. The emphasis is on stamina, tactics and technique.

Jumping is also an Olympic event, thrilling to watch. Jumpers are judged on distance and form. Each competitor is allowed three jumps. The two best scores are totaled for the final score, with sixty points each possible for distance and form. The longest jump is always awarded sixty points. In scoring style or form, all phases of the jump are observed by five judges who mark the score down from twenty points as errors are observed. Highest and lowest scores by the judges are eliminated. Emphasis is on form and the best application of aerodynamic principles.

Chapter 5

There are many safety precautions that the experienced skier abides by as a matter of course. Often his knowledge and caution have been learned as a result of trial and error, accidents and/or unpleasant experiences. These can be avoided by the beginning skier. The hazards of skiing need not be learned through chance.

If the novice observes warning signs at recreational areas and takes professional ski lessons, he has begun to tap the major sources of guidance available to him. Pamphlets from ski shops and ski and safety organizations are another source of information on equipment, winter driving, safety precautions and ski etiquette.

A course in dryland skiing and physical conditioning is the beginning skier's best insurance against hazard to himself and others. The ensuing chapter is dedicated to the philosophy that ACCIDENTS CAN BE PREVENTED.

WARM-UPS

The period of inactivity, sitting on a chair lift in very cold weather, can be very discomforting. The body may become chilled and muscles may not respond quickly. It is always advisable to warm up somewhat before skiing down, even if the weather is mild. Flinging arms forward and backward at shoulder level in a hugging movement or circling the arms vigorously similar to a pitcher's movement will increase circulation in the upper body.

Hopping the tails of the skis is an excellent warm-up for the total body. For beginning skiers, stand on the flat, arms straight while leaning on the poles placed at ski tips; hop tails to a snowplow and back together quickly; repeat ten or more times. The intermediate skier may displace the tails sideward in both directions from a traverse. Twisting, knee bends and toe touching exercises take only a few minutes and are well worth the time. Climbing is an excellent warm-up.

For the first run of the day or after lunch, one should choose a slope that does not push the skier's ability. Ski slowly, doing as many turns as possible between two points. Jump small bumps or moguls and skate to warm-up and build confidence. These suggestions are appropriate to skiers of all levels.

USE OF SKI LIFTS

There are a variety of lift devices available at ski recreational areas, all of which require special directions and precautions. The following suggestions will prevent mishaps.

Getting on and off a rope tow:

> Ski in a parallel position on the "upski" (the uphill tracks made by other skiers).
> Hold poles in the hand, away from the rope.
> Don't get too close to the person ahead of you. Space out according to the ski area's posted sign.
> Hold both hands around rope as in holding a baseball bat. An alternate position is to reach behind and grip the rope with your outside hand. The inside hand holds the rope in front. This position offers support from behind and is not so tiring to arms and shoulders. Allow the rope to pass through hands, then very gradually increase the grip on the rope until

the skis move. Body position resembles that of a water skier, knees slightly bent, leaning slightly backward; keep skis parallel.

In stepping off, decrease tension of grip and at the same time step off aggressively with one ski across the slope on the uphill edge; inside hand rests on top of the rope for balance until the other ski is moved alongside. Another method: twist both ankles to direct the skis off the upski; an extra pull on the rope just before releasing it will give the necessary momentum. Avoid allowing the rope to rise rapidly as it is released—a rope which is snapped may cause the skier behind to lose his balance.

Remember to squeeze the rope! Don't grab it suddenly or you will be likely to fall. If skiers fall on the upski in front of you, steer your skis around them or let the rope slide through your hands until they move. Don't panic and run into them. If you should fall, let go of the rope and move out of the upski as quickly as possible.

Getting on and off a T-bar or J-bar:

Ski into a parallel position on the upski. One or two persons may ride a T-bar. One person rides a J-bar.

Wait for the operator to place the bar at the level of the buttocks. If riding a T-bar alone you will be on the inside.

Keep knees slightly bent and lean back slightly. Do not sit down on the bar.

To leave the T-bar, pull yourself forward and ski off to the side. The second skier moves the bar to the side and then to the front, releasing it carefully when he and his clothing is free.

Getting on and off a poma lift (sometimes called platter-pull):

Ski into a parallel position on the upski.

The operator will hand the platter to you. Place the platter between your legs.

Bend the knees slightly and lean back; do not sit down.

To leave the poma lift, bend the knees more and move them apart in order to bring the platter to the front. Hold onto the platter until the top of the upski is reached, then release and ski off. Unlike the rope tow and most T-bars, skiers may not usually leave the poma lift at any point. Ask the operator, if in doubt.

Getting on and off a chair lift:

Ski into position for the chair. If it is a double chair, the heavier person rides on the inside (the chair closest to the tower); when riding alone ("single"), sit on the inside chair.

Keep skis parallel and hold poles in your outside hand, the hand away from the support bar, with straps off the wrist.

Watch over the shoulder which is closest to the upright bar. The bar might be in between the seats or may be on either side of the seats. Steady the chair with the free hand and sit down. Keep ski tips up.

At the top of the hill, place skis parallel on the snow, steady the chair with the inside hand and ski away. Some ski areas have signs directing partners to move in opposite directions as they leave the chair. Read and observe all signs.

Never swing your legs or cause the chair to swing or bounce. This is extremely dangerous; the cable may be bounced off the supporting towers.

There are several types of chair lifts, which require varying methods of loading and unloading. They may have a bar which closes across the skier's lap. The chair operator will open the bar as the chair approaches the awaiting skier; the bar is then swung closed by the skier himself after loading. This type of chair may have a footrest attached to the lap bar and may have a double or a single chair. Some safety bars raise and lower overhead.

When riding gondolas or other types of lifts, read directions carefully! Many serious accidents occur because people are careless and fail to follow directions. USE COMMON SENSE.

In some parts of the country, helicopters and snow planes are used as uphill conveyances. Motorized vehicles, known as "snowcats," carry large numbers of skiers into virgin ski country by a method called skijoring. The skiers hold onto a long rope or ropes and are towed along at a moderate pace.

Skijoring behind horses has been a popular sport for many years. A current trend is joring behind skimobiles, definitely not recommended for beginners. Even at moderate speed, it would be extremely dangerous to attempt skijoring behind an automobile. Tobogganing should be mentioned in this classification of thrill-seeking. Hazards of terrain and snow conditions seldom allow for any safety measure in tobogganing. Lack of common sense or rules of conduct can cause serious accidents.

The following tips for safer and more enjoyable skiing are recommended by the National Ski Patrol and the Professional Ski Instructors of America.

COURTESY

Carry your skis carefully so others are not hit by your equipment.

Wait your turn in the lift line; line-cutting is reserved for ski school classes and working ski patrolmen.

Avoid walking on ski slopes without skis. The hole left by a boot may cause a skier to fall. If necessary, walk at the edge of the slope.

Follow posted instructions at the ski area. Ask the lift operator, ski patrol or ski instructor if you don't understand.

Fill your sitzmarks. Tramp the snow with your skis to smooth the area, filling the hole and avoiding a fall for another skier.

Ski in control. Be able to stop when necessary, and be ready to avoid other skiers.

Wear ski-retaining devices to avoid loose skis. Shout a warning to those below when a ski is loose. A runaway ski is extremely dangerous and can cause serious injury.

Give way to the beginner. His control may not be as good as yours.

Do not swing or bounce lift chairs. Avoid snapping poma lift platters, T-bars or ropes. You may cause other skiers to fall off or cause lift failure.

Cooperate with the ski patrol. They will assist you and give you information about the ski area.

CONDUCT

Leave the ski lift unloading platform promptly to make room for skiers behind you.

Check skier traffic before starting. Look uphill for oncoming skiers before descending.

When overtaking another skier, the overtaker shall avoid the skier below or beyond him. He may not see you.

Let the skier know on which side you are passing. Shout "on your right" or "passing left," or "track."

A moving skier should pass at a reasonably safe distance from a stationary skier.

Stop at the side of trails or at visible locations which will not impede or block the normal passage of other skiers.

Skiers entering a main slope from a side or intersecting trail shall yield to skiers already on the slope.

Skiers approaching each other on opposite traverses shall pass to the right to avoid collision.

When arriving at the botttom of the slope, do not stand in the first runout at the end of the trail. You may be in the way of other skiers moving very fast.

SAFETY

Be physically fit. Get a good night's sleep before skiing.

Eat a good breakfast, Stop for lunch. Don't drink alcoholic beverages.

Drive safely to and from the ski area.

Dress for the weather; wear non-breakable sunglasses or goggles; use sunburn cream even on cloudy days; check for frostbite on cold days.

Use proper equipment; check release bindings often.

Follow posted instructions at ski lifts and on the slopes.

Learn trail signs: green square—easiest; blue circle, more difficult; black triangle, most difficult. Consult a ski area map for slope difficulty.

Be aware of danger spots. Red diamond sign means *extra caution.*

Obey trail closure signs. Orange or red octagonal signs mean *avalanche closure.*

Ski within your ability. Improve by taking lessons from a certified ski instructor.

Loose clothing and long hair are hazards on rope tows and ski lifts.

On ski lifts, remove straps from wrists and carry poles with points held to the back. Take straps off wrists when skiing in wooded area. The jerk caused when the ski pole basket becomes caught may dislocate a shoulder.

Keep ski tips up when riding chair lifts.

Avoid deep snow until you've learned to ski well.

When ski touring away from the ski area, check out and check back in with the ski patrol or other responsible individuals. It may be worth your life.

Ski with companions when skiing remote runs or areas. Four or more is recommended. If an accident occurs, one stays with the victim, two go for help. Mark the site with skis. Report the accident to the patrol or lift operator.

Stop skiing when you are tired or when visibility is poor. Allow sufficient time to complete your last run before the ski patrol "sweeps" the slopes.

Ski defensively; be aware of other skiers; be ready at all times to react to the unpredictable movements of beginners.

Any recreational ski area operating under forest use permit must have a voluntary or paid ski patrol. The permit requires that these patrols meet the standards of the National Ski Patrol System or its equivalent.

Patrol members may be recognized by a distinctive uniform, in most cases, a rust colored parka. These men and women are the first skiers on the slopes and the last to leave or "sweep" the hill, and they know about safety or trail hazards. First aid rooms are available, well supplied and maintained by duty personnel of the NSPS.

An injured skier should not be moved. Mark the area as an accident site. Crossed skis should be placed in the snow at least 20 feet above the victim, preferably in two places, to act as a barrier. Advice or aid from well-meaning passers-by should be ignored, since the performance of winter first aid and transportation requires specialized training. A parka may be placed over and under the victim, if movement is possible without causing further injury. The head should be lowered, unless there is a head injury, since shock will develop when any but a minor accident occurs. Removal of equipment should be left to the ski patrolman. Never remove an injured skier's ski boots.

Ski patrolmen and women not only aid in rescue and first aid, but they also promote safety and ski accident prevention. Their work results in safer recreation areas.

EXPOSURE PROBLEMS

In addition to accident hazards, there are exposure problems. These can be avoided through knowledge and application of preventive measures. They include effects of high altitude, severe temperatures, sun and wind.

Altitude or mountain sickness Whenever one ascends rapidly to an altitude greater than that to which he is accustomed, his system must adjust to the new condition. Breathing becomes more rapid in order to extract the necessary oxygen from the thinner air. The blood must adjust also by increasing its proportion of oxygen-carrying red corpuscles. In extreme cases, such as when an airplane pilot climbs thousands of feet in seconds, unconsciousness can result. The mountaineer, moving upward foot by foot, suffers less drastic but very uncomfortable symptoms. First comes general malaise and loss of appetite, followed by increasing weakness. If, by social pressure or inner resolution, the mountaineer is forced to continue the climb, he eventually becomes apathetic, nauseated, dizzy and sleepy. Symptoms of mountain sickness can occur even at relatively low altitudes. Tourists driving in automobiles to 8,000 feet sometimes feel lazy or dizzy or may experience palpitations. Climbers generally have more time to acclimatize and, except for shortness of breath, usually feel only minor effects until elevations of 14,000 feet or more are reached. However, in regions such as the Pacific Northwest where skiers dwell at sea level and ascend to over 14,000 feet on a weekend, mountain sickness of greater or lesser severity is the rule rather than the exception. Add inadequate rest, unbalanced diet (probably lacking in sufficient protein) and vigorous physical output following a long drive from sea level to 10,000 feet, and the result may well be altitude sickness.

Prevention is simple: Take it easy the first day of skiing, eat a well balanced diet and take frequent rest periods, especially after lunch. Physical conditioning before the ski season is a must.

Frostbite Frostbite is a hazard in extremely cold weather. The face, fingers and feet are affected most often. Poor circulation, poor nutrition, physical exhaustion, general illness, and wind (see chill factor chart) are some causes. Previous attacks of frostbite increase the susceptibility. The first sign that frostbite may occur is a flushed skin color which changes to white or greyish-yellow. In severe cases, blisters may appear. Pain is sometimes felt in early stages, but

WIND CHILL FACTOR CHART°
(EFFECTS OF WIND ON TEMPERATURE)

Wind Speed MPH	Local Temperature (°F)						
	32°	23°	14°	5°	−4°	−13°	−22°
	Equivalent Temperature (°F)						
Calm	32°	23°	14°	5°	−4°	−13°	−22°
5	32°	20°	10°	1°	−9°	−18°	−28°
10	29°	7°	−4°	−15°	−26°	−37°	−48°
15	18°	−1°	−13°	−25°	−37°	−49°	−61°
20	7°	−6°	−19°	−32°	−44°	−57°	−70°
25	3°	−10°	−24°	−37°	−50°	−64°	−71°
30	1°	−13°	−27°	−41°	−54°	−68°	−82°
35	−1°	−15°	−29°	−43°	−57°	−71°	−85°
Little Danger If Properly Clothed		Exposed Skin in Danger of Freezing					

°COURTESY OF SKI INDUSTRIES OF AMERICA

subsides until the part feels numb. The victim may not be aware of frostbite if it occurs on the face or on the toes.

Frostbite causes damage to the blood vessels, hemorrhage and liberation of plasma from the blood into the tissue. This causes swelling or blistering. At high altitudes, less oxygen reaches the tissues, and the warming effect of oxygen is reduced, predisposing the tissue to frostbite.

Proper clothing (dry clothing, mittens instead of gloves, covering for the ears) helps avoid frostbite. Avoid alcoholic drinks and smoking before and during exposure. If a body member becomes cold, place it against a warm body part with firm pressure. Beware of wind exposure which chills the body and reduces circulation in the extremities.

The first aid instructions given here are recommended by the American Red Cross. Never rub a frostbitten area. Severe damage can be caused to the delicate and brittle tissues. Cover the frozen area and warm gradually in a warm room; submerge the affected area in water at body temperature (90 degrees F. to 100 degrees F.), never in hot water. Do not use hot water bottle or expose the area to a heater. Any excessive heat may cause further injury.

Snow blindness When eyes are inadequately protected, they are subjected to the light reflected from the snow. This may damage the tissues of the eye and cause snow blindness. This may occur on a cloudy or brilliant day but is more likely during the spring when the days are long and the sun is high. Ultraviolet rays at high altitudes are more harmful because there is less haze in the air to absorb them. Many short repeated exposures in one day can be as damaging as continuous exposure.

The symptoms include burning or a sensation as of sand in the eyes, muscle spasms, extreme sensitivity to light or profuse watering. Sight may be affected, but this is usually temporary. Headache, weak eyes and considerable discomfort may continue for a while afterward.

Protect your eyes at all times with a good pair of dark glasses, preferably with optical quality lenses which are designed to absorb ultraviolet rays. Avoid sunglasses or goggles which obstruct your side vision. Contact lenses are not adequate.

Carry an extra pair with you for safety at all times, and never ski without some sort of eye protection. The best lens color is gray for bright days, amber for cloudy days. You can get glasses with interchangeable lenses or you can carry two pair. Don't try bizarre colors such as blue or green. This is poor protection and may damage your eyes.

If you suffer snow blindness, see a physician immediately. In the meantime, lie down, cover the eyes with cold compresses renewed every 15 to 20 minutes. Keep the eyes covered and stay out of the light.

Sunburn and windburn The face, neck and ears can be painfully burned from ultraviolet rays prevalent at high altitudes. Always carry a protective sunburn lotion so that it can be applied several times a day. Check the labels. Try to find a lotion that is a "sun block"; that is, one which will keep harmful rays from reaching the skin. Excessive exposure can cause blistering, especially of the lips. "Fever blisters" are caused by a virus but are aggravated by sunburn or exposure.

Wind, combined with loose or blowing snow, can be very irritating to the skin as well as a contributor to frostbite. A chamois or knit face-mask is welcome protection in extreme weather. Parkas which have built-in, tucked-away hoods are important accessories. A hood that can be pulled on in a jiffy can afford excellent protection, especially on a slow chairlift.

Chapter 6

WINTER DRIVING

Good skiing weather is usually bad driving weather, unfortunately. Adverse weather and road conditions exaggerate driving problems, requiring greater knowledge, skill and caution.

The driver must be aware of his physical condition. Fatigue from a physically demanding day of skiing may cause drowsiness and slow reaction time. Heavy clothing and a heated car will add to this condition. Compensate by adjusting ventilation, by making frequent rest stops, and by using the car radio or singing when alone.

VEHICLE PREPARATION

Any trip under unfavorable wintertime conditions will take longer and require special winter extras. Antifreeze should be added after inspection of the cooling system. Engine should be given a thorough tune-up at the start of cold weather. Check chains for worn areas and proper fit. Carry a snow brush and windshield ice scraper to supplement the defroster. Check windshield wipers for adequate tension and worn or streaking blades. Solvent in proper concentrate should replace water in windshield washer.

Have brakes adjusted and relined if necessary. Have the exhaust system tested for leaks. Have the electrical system checked to be sure that all lights, turn signals and battery are functioning properly. A booster cable for dead batteries is recommended equipment. Seat belts should be available for each passenger. Use all-weather lubricants in engine, transmission and differential. Check the functioning of the heater. Old-style manifold-type heaters are dangerous because of the possibility of carbon monoxide poisoning.

Carry a bag of sand and a shovel. Metallic traction mats such as AAA "Trac-Treds" are recommended for negotiating a slippery area or snow drift. Powdered bleach is excellent for using under tires on slippery areas. Carry wiping cloth, flashlight, flares, fuses, fire extinguisher, first-aid kit, blanket, tow rope and a can of aerosol engine quick-starter. Tie handkerchief to radio antenna, rear-view mirror, left door handle, or window post as a signal for help or breakdown. Ski-racks may reduce visibility through the rear window. Carry skis tail-forward, shovels to the rear, on a roof rack in order to cut down wind resistance, improve gas mileage and aid driving control.

HAZARDOUS CONDITIONS

As the driver approaches higher altitudes he will find constantly changing conditions. Fog, rain or sleet will create a hazardous driving surface. Changes in temperature are subtle, but dangerous.

Reduce speed. On an icy surface, the warmer the ice, the more slippery the driving surface. In dense fog, follow the center line very slowly; if necessary to pull off the road, make sure there is adequate space and no dropoff at the edge of the shoulder.

Stay at least twice the recommended regular driving distance behind the car in front. It takes from three to 12 times farther to stop on snow and ice than on dry pavement. Watch for stalled vehicles; never stop behind them. Drive around and stop in front, if you wish to offer help. Watch for falling rocks and animals on the road.

Use headlights freely; you may not see better, but other drivers will see you sooner. At night, drive with low beams in a fog or heavy snowstorm. High beams reflect more light back at the driver. In a day-time fog, drive with high beams to help others see you. Use flasher signals or blink stop lights when halting in a fog to warn following drivers.

Keep windshield, rear window, outside rear-view mirror and all lights clear of dirt, snow, frost, sleet and mud. In one-fifth of all fatal accidents, the driver's vision is obstructed. In two-fifths of the cases, there is rain, snow, or sleet on the windshield. Keep windshield and windows clear of fog on the inside with a clean cloth. Circulating air inside the car will reduce fogging. (The defroster blower should be used. Lowering the two back windows about an inch will help.)

Be ready psychologically when the temperature is approaching freezing. Glare ice is most hazardous when wet or near the freezing point. At 32 degrees at only 20 miles-per-hour, the braking distance on ice is over 200 feet, nearly twice as for as at zero degree F. Regardless of temperature variation, reinforced chains will reduce braking distance. Most mountainous areas require the use of chains when conditions warrant. Reinforced chains are recommended. Letting the air out of tires does not increase traction; it may even increase the tendency to skid on curves. Some areas permit snow tires as a substitution for chains. Check with the Highway Patrol.

Carbon monoxide poisoning Carbon monoxide, a colorless and odorless gas, forms a part of automobile exhaust emission. Therefore, when an auto engine is running in a confined space or backed against a snowbank, blocking the exhaust pipe, this deadly gas can be forced into the car and cause unconsciousness or death to the occupants.

Symptoms are drowsiness which lapse into unconsciousness, a cherry-red flush to the skin, shallow or no breathing at all.

Prevention is simple: Don't warm up a car in a closed garage. After backing into or parking with the car's rear end against a snowbank, be sure the exhaust pipe is not plugged with snow. Always have fresh air coming into the car with the blower or with windows down for adequate ventilation. This includes waiting in a line of traffic with someone else's exhaust blowing in your face.

If symptoms of carbon monoxide poisoning appear, call the sheriff or fire department for resuscitator equipment. Move the victim to the open air. Give artificial respiration if the victim is not breathing. Keep the victim lying down and warm until help arrives.

TIRES

Snow tires are slightly more effective than regular tires. They give 51 percent better traction on loosely packed snow. However, today's rapid snow removal makes such conditions less frequent.

Radial tires work better on ice than snow tires and are much better on dry roads than regular tires. The cost for radials is about 40 percent more than for first-line tires, but one can expect to receive at least 50 percent better tread wear.

In extreme conditions, radial studded snow tires give the best protection. These are standard snow tires with between 70 and 120 tungsten carbide studs. The metal studs dig into ice or packed snow, reducing braking distance 25 percent when used on all four wheels. There is as much as three times greater traction.

According to researchers, rubber becomes more efficient as temperatures drop while metal becomes less efficient. Therefore, at freezing, studded tires work best but near zero temperatures they are no better than regular snow tires.

Metal studs are damaging to highways and are banned in some states, while others allow studded tires but restrict their use to the winter months.

CHAINS

The universal type of chain is adjustable to about five different sizes of tires. Or you may select chains sized specifically for your tires. Individually-sized chains are more difficult to fit unless each link of cross-tie is flat and perfectly spaced. The universal type requires a chain-tightener.

Chain tighteners can be obtained from dealers. They include an all-rubber ring and a spring star (a metal ring in the center with springs spoking outward toward the chains). Carry some heavy wire to use in repairing links, to hold extra links in place or to repair the chain tightener if it should break.

The more expensive chains will have lugs welded onto the cross ties. These lugs have sharp "U" shaped prongs which project into snow and ice. Another reinforced type has twisted links in the cross tie. These dig into the snow and ice but are not as effective as ice lugs. Non-reinforced chains have flat links in the cross ties.

Examine the links for quality of construction. Observe the welding to see if the links are joined satisfactorily. Weight and thickness are of a lesser concern. Some chains are certified.

You can put chains on using various methods.

1. Hook a tire chain fastener to the chains and place over the top of the tire. As the car moves forward the chains are pulled evenly over the tire. Then fasten the inside lock at the bottom, and lock the outside lock.

2. Lay the chains out flat, back over the chains and hook the locks at the top. Hook the inside lock first.

3. Use a bumper jack to free the wheel, making the application easier.

4. Put chains on the spare tire, jack up the car and exchange tires. Do the same with the tire you have just removed. This can be an amazingly quick method, about 15 minutes if you know how to use your bumper jack.

5. Use universal tire chains which require chain tighteners. "Jiffy Tire Chains" have rigid, bent wire handles which support the inside section as you lift the chains over the tire; attachment is made on the inside with a jiffy hook. Fasten the outside lock. Additional links may be held in place by wire to prevent tire-slap. Manufacturer claims with this type, tighteners are not needed. To remove, proceed in *reverse* order.

6. Better yet, for approximately $3 you can hire someone to put them on for you.

Except with the "jiffy" type, always remove the inside lock first. Stop the car so that the hooks are positioned at the bottom of the tire. If you release the front hook first, the weight of the chains will cause them to fall off the tire onto the axle. Big trouble!

When chains are first applied, drive slowly to

allow the chains to position themselves. Centrifugal force will allow the chains to expand and loosen. Adjustments can be made and the extra links fastened with wire.

Carry a waterproof sheet, old coveralls or a storm-suit. Use the plastic gloves included in some chain sets for protection from wind. Regular gloves are too bulky.

After purchase, try tire chains on your tires before driving to snow country. Do not assume they will fit.

Apply chains the night before a storm is expected if you are staying overnight at mountain lodging.

If your car has front wheel drive the chains will do little good on the rear tires. Some automobiles cannot use tire chains because there is inadequate space between the tire and fender.

SKIDS

In a heavy rain or slush the front wheels actually leave the road. At less than 30 mph the front tires begin to lose contact with the pavement; at around 50 mph they lift up on a tough film of water and only the outer ribs are touching; at about 55 mph the front tires lose all contact; at 60 mph the front wheels can actually coast down to a full stop.

To help prevent skids, keep well below dry-road speed and pulling steadily; you need moderate power, not speed. Take curves slowly and cautiously. Avoid sudden changes in speed, gear ratio or direction. To slow down or stop, lightly "pump" the brake pedal in rapid succession, alternating on and off two or three times per second. Don't drive on the road edge or shoulder, and avoid ruts and bumps at high speed. Watch for ice patches in shaded areas and in dips. Remember, nothing entirely eliminates the possibility of skidding on snow or ice.

Once a skid has begun, the driver must not panic and slam on the brakes. This will only extend the skid; the objective is to regain traction and keep the front wheels ahead of the back wheels. If the back end of the car skids, turn in the direction of the skid. After recovery, either lightly pump the brakes to slow down or gently accelerate to continue moving. Avoid over-steering, since turning the wheel too far will whip the rear end into a skid in the opposite direction. Keep the clutch engaged or the selector lever at "D." Let up on the accelerator slowly; a sudden release might produce a braking effect which may accentuate the skid. If wheels become mired in deep snow or mud, rock the car out after first placing sand or branches or traction mats under both rear wheels. Shovel space in front of wheels to lessen the slope. Applying power slowly and steadily, shift rapidly from low to reverse and back again. Each rock should move the car a little forward or backward until the surface of the hole is packed and enough momentum is gained to move out. Keep exhaust pipe clear. Passengers should be out of the car and the car windows should be opened.

NIGHT DRIVING

The fatal accident rate at dusk and night is two-and-one-half times greater than during daylight hours. Speed should go down as the sun goes down. Watch for animals along the edge or crossing the road.

Keep alert. Don't drive when tired. Do not wear tinted glasses at night or during a night snow storm. Avoid light inside the car, such as lighting matches. The driver's eyes readjust very slowly. Don't look directly at headlights of oncoming cars. Look to the right-hand edge of the road. Depress headlights in time to prevent blinding oncoming cars, especially in case of snow reflections. Keep as far to the right as possible, when meeting a one-eyed car; it is often difficult to tell which light is out.

If you are interested in reading more about winter driving, the AAA Foundation for Traffic Safety has published (1966) a book I recommend: *Safe Winter Driving Guides* by Amos E. and Helen L. Neyhart. Also, a good film available through the Automobile Club of Southern California is *Six Deadly Skids*.

Chapter 7

Abstem   Opening the tail of the downhill ski away from the parallel position.

Airplane turn   An airborne maneuver in which legs are not retracted and a change of direction is made.

Angulation   Leaning away from the slope with the upper body in a traverse or toward the outside of a turn; the knees and hips move toward the slope.

Anticipation   Slight turning of the upper body combined with angulation toward the direction of the turn, preparatory to and affecting the initiation of the turn.

Arlberg   Mountain region of Austria which fathered the classic Arlberg and the modern Austrian Techniques; the former stresses rotation, the latter stresses reverse position.

Arlberg strap   A strap attached to the ski or binding which, when wrapped around the boot and ankle, furnishes support and keeps a loosened ski from running away.

Avalanche cord   Nylon cord of 100 feet or more, tied to skiers traveling in avalanche terrain.

Avalement (ah-vahl-mahn)   A French word for the retraction of legs and bending at the waist used to absorb bumps; in large bumps, the feet advance slightly for greater absorption.

Backward lean A movement backward to balance when decelerating.

Blocking Stopping the upper body movement by contracting the abdominal muscles, thus transferring the movement to the skis.

Boiler plate A hard sheet of ice.

Brackage (brah-kahj) A French word for steering with feet and lower leg muscles.

Camber A curved ski design from tip to tail; may refer to side or bottom curve.

Carving Ski follows the line created when the ski is edged and weighted.

Chairlift A means of uphill transportation consisting of a series of moving chairs suspended from a cable; chairs can accommodate one or two skiers.

Check A maneuver used to slow down the movement of skis.

Christy (Christies) Abbreviation for "Christiana" (derived from the town, Christiana, Norway); a basic turning maneuver in which the turn ends in a skidding phase.

Comma The angulated body position used in modern reverse-shoulder skiing.

Corn Granulated snow found in spring or warm weather, formed by alternate freezing and thawing.

Counter motion Motion around the verticle axis of the body opposite the direction of the turn.

Counter rotate A quick turning motion of one part of the body resulting in a counter action in another part of the body.

CSIA Canadian Ski Instructor's Alliance, the association of ski instructors which sets standards of instruction and certifies professional ski teachers in Canada.

CUSSA Central United States Ski Association, a division of the United States Ski Association.

Downhill One of the three basic forms of Alpine racing competition, in which skiers compete against time in a downhill run, following the natural terrain of the trail, restricted by occasional control gates.

Downhill ski In any ski maneuver, the lower ski or the one which will become the lower ski upon completion of the maneuver.

Down un-weighting A dropping of the body quickly with bending at the knees, ankles and hips; also rapidly dropping into an angulated position.

Edge Angle The angle between the bottom of the ski and the slope.

Edge control The control of the angle of the running surface of the skis to the slope.

Fall line The imaginary line marking the shortest route down a slope or the line that a falling body would follow.

FIS *Federation Internationale de Ski,* the International Ski Federation that supervises organized skiing and regulates international competition.

Flat A level spot in a ski area.

Flush An arrangement of slalom gates containing three or more closed gates in a tight series.

Forward Lean A movement forward to balance and to weight fronts of skis while accelerating; leverage.

Frozen granular Tiny crystals of frozen snow, often confused with ice.

FWSA Far West Ski Association, a division of the United States Ski Association.

Garland An exercise in which skis are alternately slipped downhill and traversed across the hill. Variations are stem garlands, side-slip garlands; a term derived from Austrian technique.

Gate An arrangement of two flags or markers through which a skier must pass in a race.

Geländesprung Airborne maneuver used to clear obstacles or bumps, performed by springing into the air, using both poles for support.

Giant slalom Basic form of Alpine racing which combines the elements of downhill and slalom competition.

Giselle Airborne maneuver in which the legs are retracted and a change of direction is made.

Gliding wedge A fundamental maneuver for controlling speed or stopping at slow speeds; from a widetrack the tails are displaced at equal angles to the line of travel, forming a slight "V"; a wider "V" position was formerly used and known as a "snowplow".

Gliding wedge turn A fundamental maneuver for turning at slow speeds, performed in the very slight "V" position; turning occurs as weight is transferred towards the outside ski along with leverage and leg steering.

Glissement (glees-mahn) A French word for the smooth sliding of relatively flat skis in contact with the snow.

Gluhwein Hot spiced wine drink, popular after skiing.

GLM Abbreviation for Graduated Length Method, a system which starts beginners on gradually increasing lengths of skis during the learning process.

Gondola A means of uphill transportation consisting of a moving enclosed car suspended from a cable.

Heel thrust Body movement resulting in the displacement of the skis with the turning point near the front of the skis.

Herringbone A basic method of climbing on skis, performed by placing each ski up on the hill in alternate steps, maintaining a "V" position and using the poles for support.

Hot dogging Performing stunts and difficult skiing maneuvers or spectacular acrobatic tricks.

Inside ski The ski describing the inside arc of a turn.

J-bar A ski lift for uphill transportation consisting of a series of "J" shaped bars attached to a moving overhead cable; the skier leans against the bar and is pulled uphill.

Jetting Rapid forward movement of skis when muscle tension is released, created by a hard edgeset at the end of a turn.

Kandahar Famous Austrian ski trail after which several international racing events are named.

Kick turn A method of reversing direction while standing on skis; performed from a stationary position.

Kurzschwingen See SHORT SWING.

Leverage Forward lean or backward weight transfer which creates turning power.

Lift line Line of skiers waiting to load onto a lift; also, a common designation for trail descending directly under the ski lift.

Long thong Long leather strap-type binding that winds around the boot, which provides support and holds the skier firmly to his skis.

Mambo A trick style of skiing with flattened skis; characterized by exaggerated, delayed counter-movement.

Mashed potatoes Heavy wet snow, usually sticky and hard to ski; also, "wet oatmeal".

Method The manner in which a "technique" is taught.

Mogul A mound of snow created by the displacement of snow as one skier after another follows a track and turns in the same spot; usually occurs on steeper slopes after a heavy snow fall.

Natural position Body weight is well balanced and is carried with the minimum strain on the muscles.

NDUSSA Northern Division, United States Ski Association.

NRSA Northern Rocky Mountain Ski Association.

NSPS National Ski Patrol System, a nationwide organization of volunteer skiers, trained in first aid and winter rescue procedures; associated with the USSA, it promotes ski safety and offers aid to disabled skiers on the slopes.

Outside ski The ski on the outside arc of a turn.

Parallel christy An advanced turn in which both skis remain together throughout the entire execution of the turn.

Piste A ski trail (a term more often used in Europe).

PNSA Pacific Northwest Ski Association.

Platter-pull See POMA LIFT.

Poma lift Means of uphill transportation, consisting of a disc affixed to a long steel bar and cable; the skier straddles the disc and is pulled uphill.

Powder Snow found after a fresh snowfall, composed of light, dry flakes.

Pre-jump Similar to a *Geländesprung;* skis are lifted into the air on the uphill side of a bump or mogul, before the crest is reached; skier lands on the smooth, downhill side of a bump.

Release binding Modern mechanism for affixing the boot to the ski; designed to permit the boot to be thrown free of the ski under excess stress.

Reverse shoulder An exaggerated style of skiing in which the upper body faces to the outside of the turn, and the lower body twists in opposition to the upper body, giving a "reverse shoulder" appearance.

Rising motion Slow rising, resulting in change of body position; not used for unweighting.

RMD Rocky Mountain Division of the United States Ski Association.

Reploiment (re-plwa-mahn) A French word for the gentle version of the down unweighting phase of *avalement*.

Rope tow Moving rope, usually operated by a gasoline engine; the skier grasps the rope and is pulled uphill.

Rotation Classic Arlberg style of skiing in which a turn is initiated by a rotating motion of the shoulders and upper body in the direction of the turn; the lower body follows the action of the upper body toward the inside of the turn; a motion around the verticle axis of the body in the direction of the turn.

Reuel christy Advanced maneuver in which the outside ski is lifted high off the snow as the turn is executed on the inside ski.

Ruade Moving, turning maneuver performer by hopping the ski tails off the snow and pivoting around on the tips; especially useful in deep snow or on steep slopes; developed in the French technique.

Rücklage Literally a "backward leaning" or shifting of the weight; body position which places the center of gravity of the skier behind the heels.

Safety binding A misnomer; see RELEASE BINDINGS.

Schmieren Style of skiing keeping skis flattened while turning; edges are not used; little perceptible lift, very little turning power. Also known as "tip-drifted christy."

Schuss Skiing straight down the fall line without turns or checks.

Short swing Advanced skiing style utilizing a continuous series of short parallel turns down the fall-line, unbroken by traverses; also known as Kurzschwingen or Wedeln. In short swing there is a more definite edgeset and anticipation.

Sideslip Slipping the skis sideways down a slope by releasing the edging.

Sinking Motion Slow down-motion used as a preparation for an up or rising motion.

Sitzmark Impression made in the snow by a fallen skier; also known as "bathtub."

"Ski!" Warning cry, indicating that a loose ski is coming down the hill.

Ski angle Angle between the ski and the fall line.

Ski position Relative position of one ski to the other, open, closed, stemmed or advanced.

Skidding Action of the tail moving laterally more than the tip.

Slalom Basic form of Alpine competition in which a racer must descend a course marked by a series of slalom gates, set singly or in combinations, passing through each gate successively.

Sliding Action of running on skis in the direction of tips on edges or flat ski.

Slipping Action of movement sideways as in vertical sideslip, forward sideslip and gliding wedge.

Snow bunny A new or beginner skier; a novice.

Split rotation Turn initiated within a confined, short or partial rotation; as the skis start the turn, a reverse shoulder motion continues the turn, finishing with a follow through body motion in the direction of the turn.

Spring conditions Snow reporting term used to designate temperature variations; surface characteristics change continually from ice or granular in the early morning to granular, corn or "mashed potatoes" at midday, back to frozen granular or ice as the temperature drops again.

SRSA Southern Rocky Mountain Ski Association; a division of the United States Ski Association.

Steering action Turning power resulting from a twisting of the feet and a forward, lateral and torsional movement of the knees.

Stem An opening of one or both tails of the skis away from the parallel position.

Stem christy An intermediate turn in which one ski is stemmed to facilitate weight shift; at the start and completion of the turn, the skis are parallel.

T-bar Ski lift for uphill transportation, consisting of a series of T-shaped bars attached to a moving overhead cable; two skiers lean against the cross bars and are pulled uphill.

Technique The manner in which mechanical details are treated or used to describe a skiing system.

Terrain Contours of the slope and steepness.

Total motion Body is never locked in one position but moves smoothly from one movement to another.

Track Path of skis; verbal expression of warning, like "fore" in golf—"Here I come."

Traverse Travel across a slope; descent at an angle to the fall line.

Turntable Swiveling plate incorporated into a binding, usually under the boot heel to facilitate the release of the boot in a fall.

Ullr Ancient Norse god of winter.

Uphill ski In any ski maneuver, the ski which is on the uphill side of the skier.

Upski Path or grooves made by skiers traveling uphill on T-bar, rope tow or poma lift.

Unweighting Reduction or elimination of the skier's weight against the snow; types of unweighting are up-unweighting, down-unweighting, passive unweighting when skiing over bumps in terrain, and rebounding unweighting from edge set.

Up-unweighting Extension of the body upwards resulting in a reduction of the skier's weight on the snow; the action of moving from an angulated position to an extended one will unweigh the ski.

USEASA United States Eastern Amateur Ski Association, a division of the United States Ski Association.

USSA United States Ski Association; the parent organization of organized skiing in America, a member of the FIS. It has seven regional divisions throughout the country.

Vorlage Forward leaning or shifting of the weight; a body position placing the center of gravity of the skier ahead of the ball of the foot.

Warp Lateral twist in a ski.

Wedeln See SHORT SWING.

Weighting Act of applying weight to the skis.

Weight transfer Transfer of body weight from one ski to the other.

Wide track Wide stance used by beginners to acquire greater stability; used by experts when skiing the upper limits of one's ability at speed and in difficult terrain.

RECOMMENDED READING

Joubert, Georges and Jean Vuarnet, *How to Ski the New French Way,* The Dial Press, Inc., New York, 1967.

Joubert, Georges, *Teach Yourself to Ski,* Aspen Ski Masters, P.O. Box 3071, Aspen, Colorado 81611.

Neyhart, Amos E. and Helen L. Neyhart, *Safe Winter Driving Guides,* AAA Foundation for Traffic Safety, 1966.

Ski (Incorporating: *Ski Life)* Universal Publishing and Distributing Corp., 235 East 45th St., New York, N.Y. 10017.

Skiing, Subscription Service Office, P.O. Box 1098, Flushing, New York 11325.

Twardokens, George, *Skiing,* Goodyear Publishing Co., Inc., Pacific Palisades, Calif. 90272, 1971.

Witherell, Warren, *How the Racers Ski,* W. W. Norton & Company, Inc., New York, 1972.